Building AI Agents: A Developer's Guide to Building Intelligent Systems with 10 Cutting-Edge Tools

Luca Randall

ii

Preface

In recent years, artificial intelligence has transcended traditional boundaries, evolving from narrowly focused applications into sophisticated, autonomous systems capable of learning, adapting, and making decisions on their own. "Building AI Agents: A Developer's Guide to Building Intelligent Systems with 10 Cutting-Edge Tools" is a comprehensive resource designed to equip developers, engineers, and AI enthusiasts with the knowledge and practical skills needed to design, build, and deploy intelligent agents that operate at scale.

This book emerged from the growing need to bridge the gap between the theoretical underpinnings of AI and real-world application. As the capabilities of AI agents have expanded—from simple chatbots to complex multi-agent systems orchestrating entire workflows—the challenge has shifted from merely understanding how AI works to mastering how to create systems that are robust, scalable, and ethically sound.

Throughout these pages, you will find a detailed exploration of foundational concepts, a deep dive into a suite of advanced tools, and practical guidance on integrating these tools into cohesive, real-world systems. Whether you're building a personal assistant, automating business processes, or pioneering new applications in emerging fields, this guide offers step-by-step tutorials, complete with code examples and real-world case studies, that make even the most advanced topics accessible.

The book is structured to take you on a journey from setting up your development environment to deploying and maintaining autonomous AI agents in production. Early chapters introduce core concepts and terminology, ensuring that you have a solid grounding before progressing to more complex architectures and advanced topics such as continuous learning, ethical considerations, and future trends in AI agent development.

One of the unique aspects of this book is its practical orientation. Every concept is illustrated with detailed examples and actionable code snippets, enabling you to translate theory into practice immediately. The content is designed to be both comprehensive and approachable, blending technical depth with a conversational tone that invites you to explore, experiment, and ultimately innovate.

As you work through the chapters, you'll discover not only how to harness current technologies like LangChain, CrewAI, AutoGen, and Semantic Kernel but also how to envision the future of autonomous systems. The strategies, techniques, and best practices presented here are drawn from both cutting-edge research and real-world experience, ensuring that you are well-prepared to tackle the challenges of developing intelligent, autonomous agents in today's dynamic digital landscape.

Whether you're a seasoned developer looking to expand your expertise or a curious newcomer eager to delve into the world of AI agents, "Building AI Agents" is your roadmap to transforming abstract ideas into powerful, practical systems. Welcome to the future of intelligent automation. Enjoy the journey, and may your path be filled with innovation and discovery.

TABLE OF CONTENTS

Introduction

Welcome to *Building AI Agents: A Developer's Guide to Building Intelligent Systems with 10 Cutting-Edge Tools*. In this introductory chapter, we'll embark on a journey through the exciting landscape of AI agents and autonomous systems. Whether you're a seasoned developer or someone curious about the future of intelligent technology, this chapter lays the foundation for understanding what AI agents are, how they evolved, and the impact they have on our world today. We'll also walk through how the book is organized and what you can expect to learn, ensuring that you feel both informed and inspired as you dive into the chapters ahead.

Overview of AI Agents and Autonomous Systems

Imagine having a personal assistant that not only schedules your appointments but also anticipates your needs, adapts to your style, and even executes tasks without needing to be told every detail. AI agents are, in many ways, like that ideal personal assistant—but for digital and complex tasks. At their core, AI agents are systems designed to act autonomously. They receive high-level goals and then break these down into manageable subtasks, executing them iteratively to achieve the desired outcome.

Autonomous systems powered by artificial intelligence can be as simple as a chatbot that answers customer service queries or as complex as a network of agents collaborating to manage an entire data center. The common thread is their ability to operate independently once given a directive, continuously learning and adapting based on the context of the task at hand.

In today's digital era, these intelligent systems are becoming indispensable across industries. From automating routine operations in businesses to enabling breakthrough innovations in healthcare, finance, and even creative fields, AI agents are shaping how we interact with technology and transforming the very fabric of work.

The Evolution and Impact of Intelligent Agents

The concept of intelligent agents isn't new—think back to early experiments in artificial intelligence during the mid-20th century, where researchers dreamt of machines that could mimic human reasoning. Over the decades, advancements in machine learning, neural networks, and more recently, large language models (LLMs), have transformed those early dreams into reality.

Today, AI agents have evolved from simple scripted bots to dynamic systems capable of processing natural language, understanding context, and executing complex multi-step tasks. This evolution has been driven by several key factors:

- **Technological Breakthroughs:** The rise of deep learning and the availability of massive datasets have allowed AI agents to improve their understanding and performance exponentially. Imagine the leap from a basic calculator to a smartphone that understands your voice and learns your habits.
- **Computational Power:** With the advent of GPUs and cloud computing, it's now possible to run sophisticated models that once took weeks to train in a matter of hours. This has opened the door for real-time applications of AI agents.
- **Open-Source Collaboration:** The growth of open-source communities has accelerated innovation. Frameworks like LangChain, AutoGen, and others have democratized access to advanced AI technologies, enabling developers around the world to build on each other's work.

The impact of these developments is profound. Businesses now leverage AI agents to reduce operational costs, enhance customer experiences, and unlock new levels of productivity. For instance, consider how an autonomous agent might streamline your daily workflow—automating repetitive tasks, providing intelligent insights, and even handling critical decision-making processes. On a societal level, the integration of AI agents into various sectors is not only changing the way we work but also reshaping entire industries, influencing job roles, and redefining productivity metrics.

Yet, as with any transformative technology, there are challenges. Issues like ethical considerations, data privacy, and security come to the forefront as AI agents become more autonomous. Balancing innovation with responsible use is a key theme we'll explore throughout this book.

How This Book is Organized & What You'll Learn

This guide is structured to be as comprehensive as it is practical, ensuring that by the end of it, you're not only familiar with the theoretical underpinnings of AI agents but also equipped with hands-on knowledge to build your own intelligent systems.

What You'll Find in This Book

- **Foundational Concepts:**
  We begin with a solid introduction to the basics of AI agents and autonomous systems. You'll learn about the core principles, key terminologies, and the evolution that has brought us to the current state of the technology.
- **Tool-Specific Deep Dives:**
  The heart of this book lies in its exploration of 10 cutting-edge AI agent tools. Each tool is presented in its own dedicated section, where we cover:
  - What the tool is and its primary purpose.
  - The strengths and unique capabilities that set it apart.
  - Real-world use cases and scenarios where it shines.
  - How it integrates with other systems and frameworks.

  This structure is designed to give you both a broad overview and deep technical insights, making it easier to decide which tool fits your specific project needs.

- **Architecting Intelligent Systems:**
  Beyond individual tools, we also discuss how to integrate them into a cohesive, robust system. This includes system design strategies, workflow management, and considerations for scaling your solutions in real-world applications.
- **Practical Development Strategies:**
  From setting up your development environment to deploying and monitoring your AI agents, practical chapters are packed with step-by-step guidance. While we refrain from diving into code at this early stage, later chapters will provide hands-on projects that bring theory to practice.
- **Advanced Topics and Best Practices:**
  As you progress, you'll encounter discussions on more advanced

topics such as security, ethical implications, and performance optimization. These chapters are designed to help you think beyond the basics and consider the broader impacts of your work.

- **Future Trends:**
  The world of AI is evolving at breakneck speed. We'll look at emerging trends and technologies that could shape the future of AI agents, ensuring that you stay ahead of the curve.

Our Approach

Throughout the book, we strive for a tone that's both conversational and tutorial-driven. We want you to feel like you're having a guided conversation with an experienced mentor rather than reading through a dry technical manual. Expect relatable analogies and personal insights that help demystify complex concepts. For example, building an AI agent might be compared to assembling a team for a challenging project—each member (or tool) has a unique role, and success depends on how well you coordinate and leverage these strengths.

We'll begin with the "why" before delving into the "how." This ensures that you have a clear understanding of the purpose and potential of AI agents before getting into the nitty-gritty details of implementation.

Why This Book Matters

In an era where technology is reshaping every aspect of our lives, understanding and harnessing AI agents is more than just a technical skill— it's a strategic advantage. Whether you're looking to innovate within your organization, build a startup, or simply explore new horizons in programming, this book offers a roadmap to mastering one of the most exciting fields in technology today.

By the end of this journey, you'll be well-versed in the key frameworks and tools that power intelligent agents, and you'll be prepared to design, build, and deploy systems that can operate autonomously. The skills you acquire here will not only enhance your technical repertoire but also empower you to lead the charge in the next wave of technological innovation.

In the chapters that follow, we'll explore each tool and concept in depth, providing you with the insights and practical guidance needed to turn your ideas into reality. So, buckle up and get ready to dive into the fascinating world of AI agents—a world where machines learn, adapt, and collaborate to solve problems in ways we once only dreamed possible.

Chapter 1: Foundations of AI Agents

In this chapter, we lay the groundwork for everything you'll learn about AI agents. We start by exploring what these agents are, delve into the key concepts that power them, examine various design patterns and architectures that guide their development, and discuss the critical roles of data integration, memory, and context. Finally, we address the ethical, security, and governance considerations that come with deploying such transformative technologies. Let's dive in.

1.1 What Are AI Agents?

AI agents are autonomous software systems that carry out tasks or achieve goals with minimal human intervention. They combine advanced algorithms, machine learning, and decision-making capabilities to analyze information, make informed choices, and execute actions—all while adapting to new data and changing environments.

At their core, AI agents function by receiving a high-level objective and then breaking it down into smaller, manageable tasks. Think of them as a highly efficient team of digital assistants, each with a specific role. For instance, an AI agent designed for customer support might handle initial inquiries, escalate complex issues to a human, and learn from each interaction to improve its responses over time.

A practical way to understand AI agents is to consider how modern navigation apps work. Much like how a navigation system gathers real-time traffic data, computes the fastest route, and updates the route dynamically if conditions change, an AI agent continually processes incoming information, applies learned patterns, and adjusts its strategy on the fly. This ability to operate both reactively and proactively is what distinguishes true autonomous agents from simple automated scripts.

Modern AI agents leverage the power of large language models (LLMs) and other deep learning techniques. LLMs, for example, enable these agents to understand and generate natural language, making interactions with users feel more intuitive and human-like. This is crucial in applications like chatbots, virtual assistants, or any scenario where nuanced communication is key. By integrating LLMs, AI agents can interpret complex instructions, maintain context over a series of interactions, and even predict user needs based on historical data.

Another significant aspect of AI agents is their capacity to operate in multi-agent systems. In these environments, several AI agents work collaboratively, each handling distinct parts of a larger task. Imagine a production line in a factory: one agent might be responsible for quality control, another for inventory management, and yet another for logistics. When these agents communicate and coordinate effectively, the entire system becomes more efficient and capable of tackling complex, multifaceted problems.

Underpinning all these capabilities are sophisticated design patterns and architectures that ensure reliability, scalability, and adaptability. Many AI agents are built using modular components, which not only streamline development but also allow for easy upgrades and maintenance. This modularity means you can integrate a new tool or upgrade an existing one without having to rebuild the entire system—a concept that mirrors the flexibility of modern software engineering practices.

The decision-making process in AI agents typically involves a feedback loop. Once an agent acts, it evaluates the outcome and learns from any discrepancies between expected and actual results. This iterative learning process is central to the concept of reinforcement learning, where agents gradually improve their performance by experimenting, receiving feedback, and adjusting their strategies accordingly.

In summary, AI agents represent a convergence of multiple advanced technologies: autonomous decision-making, natural language processing, machine learning, and system orchestration. They are designed to reduce the need for constant human oversight by automating complex tasks, enabling faster, more efficient workflows in areas ranging from customer service to software development and beyond. As you progress through this book, you'll see how these principles are applied practically using cutting-edge tools, transforming abstract concepts into real-world, deployable systems.

1.2 Key Concepts: LLMs, Multi-Agent Systems, and Agent Orchestration

Large Language Models (LLMs), multi-agent systems, and agent orchestration are foundational concepts that together enable the creation of intelligent, self-directing systems.

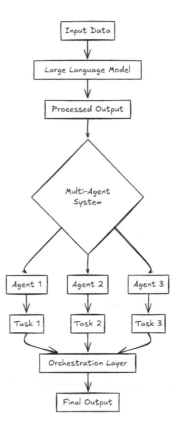

Large Language Models (LLMs)

LLMs are at the heart of modern AI agents. These models are trained on enormous amounts of text data, enabling them to understand context, generate human-like language, and even perform reasoning tasks. What makes LLMs particularly powerful is their ability to capture subtle linguistic nuances and deliver contextually relevant outputs. This means they can translate high-level instructions into actionable tasks, forming the backbone for natural language interfaces in AI agents.

Consider an LLM as a highly skilled translator that doesn't merely convert words from one language to another but understands intent, tone, and context. When an AI agent receives a command, the LLM processes this input, interprets the underlying requirements, and produces a coherent response or triggers subsequent actions. This capability has fueled a wide array of applications, from chatbots that handle customer service to systems that generate code snippets from textual descriptions.

Beyond language generation, LLMs also empower agents with memory and contextual awareness. By maintaining a short-term memory of recent interactions and accessing a larger knowledge base, these models can offer consistent and context-rich responses over extended dialogues. This integration of language understanding with contextual continuity is a key factor that makes LLM-powered systems both robust and versatile.

Multi-Agent Systems

In many real-world scenarios, a single AI agent might not be enough to handle the complexity of a task. That's where multi-agent systems come in. These systems consist of several autonomous agents that work concurrently, each specialized in a particular function, yet designed to collaborate toward a common goal.

Imagine a busy restaurant where different staff members—chefs, waiters, and managers—each perform specific roles. In a multi-agent system, one agent might be responsible for processing user queries, another for fetching and integrating data from external sources, and yet another for managing decision-making based on cumulative insights. The strength of this approach lies in its ability to decompose complex tasks into simpler, parallel processes, enhancing overall efficiency and resilience.

From a development standpoint, multi-agent systems introduce both opportunities and challenges. They allow developers to modularize tasks, making systems easier to build, test, and scale. However, they also require careful planning regarding communication protocols, conflict resolution, and overall system coordination. The benefits, however, are substantial—when agents work together seamlessly, the result is an intelligent system that can handle intricate workflows, adapt to dynamic environments, and maintain operational integrity even if one part of the system encounters issues.

Agent Orchestration

While multi-agent systems provide the structure for distributed task handling, agent orchestration is the mechanism that coordinates their efforts. Think of orchestration as the conductor of an orchestra, ensuring that each instrument (or agent) plays in harmony to create a symphony. Without proper orchestration, even highly capable agents might work at cross purposes, leading to inefficiencies or outright failures.

Effective orchestration involves setting clear protocols for how agents communicate, share data, and hand off tasks. It ensures that the output of one agent becomes the seamless input for another, creating a fluid chain of operations that collectively achieve complex objectives. In practice, orchestration might involve a central controller or a decentralized set of rules that guide interactions. The goal is always to achieve a balance—enabling agents to operate autonomously while ensuring they remain aligned with the system's overall objectives.

One practical approach to orchestration is using middleware or dedicated frameworks that manage the lifecycle of each agent. These systems handle tasks such as scheduling, error handling, and performance monitoring, thereby relieving developers from reinventing the wheel for every new project. The result is a scalable, maintainable, and efficient system where every agent contributes optimally.

In summary, understanding these three key concepts is critical for anyone looking to build intelligent AI systems. LLMs provide the conversational intelligence and contextual awareness that power the decision-making process; multi-agent systems break down complex tasks into manageable, collaborative components; and effective agent orchestration ensures that these components work together harmoniously. As you delve deeper into the following chapters, keep these concepts in mind—they serve as the bedrock upon which robust and innovative AI agent systems are built.

1.3 Design Patterns and Architectures for Autonomous Systems

When building autonomous systems, thoughtful design patterns and architectures aren't just nice-to-have—they're essential. They ensure that your AI agents are not only effective and scalable but also maintainable over time. In this section, we'll explore a few key architectural paradigms and design patterns that underpin robust autonomous systems, along with expert commentary on their practical implications.

Modular Architecture: Building with Interchangeable Components

Modularity is one of the fundamental principles in software engineering, and it plays an equally critical role in autonomous systems. Imagine constructing a machine from LEGO bricks—each brick represents a specific functionality, and you can swap them out without rebuilding the entire structure. In the context of AI agents, modular architecture means designing your system as a collection of loosely coupled components. Each module handles a discrete task, such as natural language understanding, data retrieval, decision-making, or interfacing with external systems.

Pipeline and Chaining Patterns: Sequential Processing for Complex Tasks

Many autonomous systems operate like assembly lines, where each stage processes input and passes the result to the next component. This pipeline or chaining pattern is particularly useful when dealing with sequential tasks. For example, an AI agent might first process user input using an LLM, then extract relevant data, and finally trigger an appropriate action based on the processed data.

Imagine a manufacturing process where raw materials are refined step-by-step into a finished product. Similarly, a well-designed pipeline ensures that each "station" or module adds value to the overall process. This pattern minimizes redundancy by allowing each component to specialize, leading to more predictable and efficient performance.

Reactive vs. Proactive Patterns: Responding to vs. Anticipating Needs

Autonomous systems can be designed to either react to events as they occur or to anticipate future conditions and act accordingly. Reactive patterns are straightforward—agents monitor their environment and respond immediately when a specific event or input is detected. This is akin to a thermostat that turns the heating on when it senses a drop in temperature.

On the other hand, proactive patterns involve forecasting and planning. These systems analyze historical data and trends to anticipate potential issues before they arise, thereby enabling preemptive action. For instance, an AI agent managing network security might predict a possible breach based on unusual activity patterns and take preventive measures.

Hybrid Architectures: Combining Rule-Based and Learning-Based Approaches

No single design pattern can address every challenge faced by autonomous systems. Hybrid architectures combine traditional rule-based systems with learning-based components, marrying the reliability of predefined rules with the adaptability of machine learning. In practice, this means embedding domain-specific logic (the rule-based part) alongside an AI's capacity to learn from data and refine its responses over time.

Real-World Analogy:
Think of a seasoned professional who relies on established best practices (the rule-based approach) while also adapting to new information and trends (the learning-based approach). This balance ensures that the system is both robust and flexible.

Distributed Architectures: Scaling Out for Performance and Resilience

As autonomous systems grow in complexity, a distributed architecture becomes vital. This approach involves spreading computational tasks across multiple nodes or agents, which work in parallel to handle large volumes of data or complex operations. Distributed systems can reduce bottlenecks and improve reliability, since the failure of one node doesn't bring the whole system down.

Practical Insight:
Consider how large-scale e-commerce platforms manage traffic during peak shopping seasons by distributing workload across servers. Similarly, distributed AI systems harness parallel processing to boost performance and ensure continuity, even in the face of individual component failures.

Communication and Coordination: The Role of Orchestration

At the heart of any multi-agent system lies effective orchestration. It's not enough to have several well-designed modules; these modules must communicate and coordinate seamlessly. Orchestration frameworks handle task scheduling, inter-agent communication, error handling, and synchronization of data across the system. This coordination ensures that each agent's output is timely and relevant, thereby achieving the overarching system goals.

Bringing It All Together

Design patterns and architectures are the backbone of autonomous systems. By employing modular designs, sequential pipelines, and distributed architectures, developers can create systems that are not only powerful and scalable but also resilient and adaptable. Whether you're designing a system that reacts instantly to user inputs or one that proactively anticipates future needs, understanding these patterns is crucial.

In the chapters ahead, we'll see how these architectural principles are applied practically through our suite of AI agent tools. With this foundational knowledge, you'll be well-equipped to design, build, and orchestrate intelligent systems that can stand up to real-world challenges.

1.4 Data Integration, Memory, and Context in Intelligent Agents

Data integration, memory, and context are not just technical add-ons—they're essential ingredients that empower AI agents to operate intelligently and adaptively in real-world environments. Let's break down these concepts to understand how they work together to create truly capable systems.

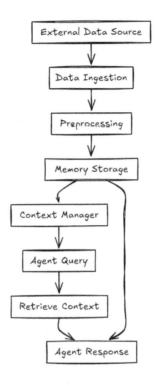

Data Integration: Gathering the Pieces

In any complex task, data is rarely stored in one neat package. Instead, it's scattered across multiple databases, APIs, documents, and real-time feeds. Data integration is the process of aggregating these disparate sources into a coherent, unified dataset that an AI agent can use. Imagine piecing together a jigsaw puzzle where each piece comes from a different box; without integration, the complete picture remains elusive.

For AI agents, effective data integration means they can pull in relevant information—be it user history, market trends, sensor data, or even unstructured text from various sources—and use it to inform their actions. This unified view of data ensures that the agent makes decisions based on a comprehensive understanding of its environment, rather than operating in isolated silos.

Memory: Retaining and Reusing Information

Once data is integrated, an intelligent agent must be able to remember past interactions and learn from them. Memory in AI systems is analogous to human memory—it enables the agent to retain context over time and make decisions that are informed by previous experiences.

There are two primary types of memory in intelligent agents:

- **Short-Term Memory:** This allows an agent to keep track of the current conversation or task. For example, during a dialogue with a user, an agent's short-term memory helps maintain context, so responses remain relevant even as the conversation evolves.
- **Long-Term Memory:** This is used for storing accumulated knowledge over extended periods. Long-term memory can include historical user data, previous decisions, or outcomes of past interactions. It provides a basis for learning, adaptation, and even personalization.

Effective memory management is crucial. Without it, an AI agent would have to treat every interaction as a new, isolated event, leading to inefficiencies and potential misinterpretations. By contrast, well-implemented memory systems allow agents to build a narrative over time, enabling smoother, more coherent interactions.

Context: The Lens of Understanding

Context acts as the lens through which all data and memory are interpreted. It provides the background that transforms raw data into meaningful information. When an AI agent understands context, it can discern not just what is being said, but why it matters. For example, the same piece of data might have different implications depending on whether it's part of a customer complaint or a routine inquiry.

Context comes in several forms:

- **Temporal Context:** Understanding the sequence and timing of events. This allows agents to prioritize recent information or notice patterns over time.
- **Situational Context:** Recognizing the current state of the environment or the user's situation. This might include location, current tasks, or even emotional tone.
- **Historical Context:** Drawing on long-term memory to provide background information that informs current decisions. This might involve user preferences, past behaviors, or previous system states.

Integrating context with data and memory transforms an AI agent from a reactive machine into a proactive and intelligent system. It's the difference between a device that merely follows instructions and one that understands the broader picture, enabling it to make nuanced decisions and predictions.

The Interplay: Creating a Cohesive System

When you combine data integration, memory, and context, you create a synergistic effect that greatly enhances an AI agent's capabilities. Data integration ensures that the agent has all the relevant information at its fingertips. Memory allows it to learn and adapt based on past experiences. Context provides the framework to interpret both new and old data meaningfully.

Imagine planning a road trip: data integration is like gathering maps, weather forecasts, and traffic reports; memory is recalling previous trips and lessons learned; and context is understanding the current road conditions and your own travel preferences. Together, these elements enable you to plan a smoother, more enjoyable journey. Similarly, in AI agents, the interplay of these components leads to systems that are more accurate, responsive, and adaptable.

As we continue through this book, remember that data integration, memory, and context are not isolated technical challenges—they are the core enablers of intelligent behavior. These elements allow AI agents to evolve from simple tools into dynamic systems capable of learning, adapting, and even anticipating future needs. Understanding and leveraging these concepts is key to building autonomous systems that are not only powerful and efficient but also truly intelligent.

By mastering these foundational aspects, you're setting the stage for developing sophisticated AI agents that can handle real-world complexities with finesse. This deep understanding will empower you to design systems that are responsive, reliable, and capable of creating lasting value in any application you pursue.

1.5 Ethical, Security, and Governance Considerations

Ethical, security, and governance issues are integral to the development and deployment of autonomous AI agents. As these systems gain more autonomy and influence over decision-making processes, it becomes essential to address these considerations head-on. In this section, we explore these critical aspects, offering practical insights and expert commentary to guide you through the responsibilities and challenges associated with building intelligent systems.

Ethical Considerations

Autonomous AI agents are increasingly involved in making decisions that affect human lives. This raises several ethical concerns that must be addressed during both the design and deployment stages.

- **Transparency and Accountability:**
  Users and stakeholders need to understand how decisions are made by AI agents. This transparency is key to fostering trust and ensuring accountability. Explainable AI (XAI) techniques are vital here, providing clear insights into the agent's reasoning process. Clear documentation and open communication about the limitations and intended use of the agent can help mitigate potential misunderstandings or misuse.
  Practical Tip: Incorporate audit logs and user-friendly explanations of the decision process so that both developers and end-users can trace how outcomes were achieved.
- **Autonomy vs. Control:**
  While the power of autonomous agents lies in their ability to operate independently, this autonomy also raises ethical questions about control and oversight. It's important to strike a balance where agents are given sufficient freedom to operate efficiently, yet remain under human supervision when necessary. Designing systems with fail-safes and intervention points can ensure that the final decision-making authority remains with human operators, especially in high-stakes applications.

Security Considerations

Security is paramount when dealing with autonomous systems that often interact with sensitive data and critical infrastructure. Robust security measures must be woven into every layer of the system to prevent unauthorized access and potential abuse.

- **Data Protection:**
  Autonomous agents typically integrate and process large volumes of data from diverse sources. Ensuring the privacy and integrity of this data is non-negotiable. Techniques such as encryption, secure data

storage, and strict access controls should be standard practice. Data anonymization and regular audits further enhance security by limiting exposure to sensitive information.

- **System Resilience and Robustness:**
Security isn't just about protecting data—it's also about ensuring that the system can withstand attacks or failures. Implementing redundancies, continuous monitoring, and automated alert systems can help detect and mitigate potential threats in real time. An effective incident response plan is crucial for addressing vulnerabilities quickly before they can be exploited.
Practical Insight: Regular penetration testing and code reviews are essential for maintaining a secure AI environment. They allow developers to identify and patch vulnerabilities before they become critical issues.

- **User Authentication and Authorization:**
With multiple agents interacting with various systems and databases, ensuring that each agent has the appropriate level of access is vital. Multi-factor authentication, role-based access control, and least-privilege principles help prevent unauthorized actions and ensure that each agent's operations are traceable and secure.

Governance Considerations

Governance involves the policies, standards, and oversight mechanisms that guide the development, deployment, and ongoing management of AI agents. Good governance is key to ensuring that these systems operate safely, ethically, and effectively over their entire lifecycle.

- **Regulatory Compliance:**
Autonomous AI systems must comply with existing laws and regulations, which can vary widely across industries and regions. This means staying informed about data protection laws, consumer rights, and emerging standards specific to AI technologies.
Expert Tip: Collaborate with legal experts to ensure that your AI systems are compliant with all relevant regulations, and be prepared to adapt as legal frameworks evolve.

- **Ethical Governance and Oversight:**
Beyond legal requirements, there is a need for ethical oversight to guide decision-making and risk management. Establishing internal review boards or ethics committees can provide ongoing scrutiny and guidance. This governance should be proactive, involving periodic audits and the incorporation of stakeholder feedback to ensure the

system remains aligned with societal values.

Practical Insight: Transparency in governance builds public trust. Sharing policies and audit results, while respecting proprietary boundaries, can foster a more informed dialogue about the responsible use of AI.

- **Operational Governance and Maintenance:**
Governance extends to how the AI agent is managed on a day-to-day basis. This includes not only monitoring system performance and security but also ensuring that the system's objectives remain aligned with business goals and ethical standards. Continuous improvement processes, such as iterative reviews and user feedback mechanisms, are critical to long-term success.

Integrating Ethical, Security, and Governance Frameworks

To build truly autonomous and reliable AI agents, ethical, security, and governance considerations must be integrated from the very beginning of the development process. They should not be an afterthought but a foundational part of the system's design. By doing so, you not only safeguard against potential risks but also enhance the system's credibility and user trust.

- **Holistic Approach:**
Treat these considerations as interconnected rather than isolated challenges. For instance, a transparent governance framework can improve both security practices and ethical accountability, while robust security measures can support compliance with ethical and regulatory standards.
- **Stakeholder Engagement:**
Engage with diverse stakeholders—including end-users, legal experts, and cybersecurity professionals—to ensure that the AI agent meets all necessary standards and expectations. This collaborative approach can lead to more resilient, well-rounded systems.
- **Continuous Evaluation:**
The landscape of AI is rapidly evolving, and so are the associated risks. Regular reviews and updates of your ethical, security, and governance frameworks are essential. Incorporating new findings, emerging technologies, and regulatory changes into your system's design helps maintain its relevance and safety.

Ethical, security, and governance considerations are not merely boxes to be checked; they are critical dimensions that define the trustworthiness and long-term viability of autonomous AI systems. By taking a proactive, integrated approach to these issues, developers can build intelligent agents that not only perform well but do so responsibly and securely.

In the chapters ahead, as you start to implement and deploy AI agents, remember that these frameworks will serve as your guiding principles, ensuring that your systems are not just innovative, but also ethical, secure, and sustainable. This foundation is essential for fostering an environment where technology and society can benefit together from the transformative power of AI.

Chapter 2: Deep Dive into the 10 Tools

In this chapter, we'll explore each of the 10 cutting-edge tools that form the backbone of modern AI agent development. By examining the core components, practical use cases, and real-world applications of these tools, you'll gain a comprehensive understanding of how to leverage them effectively. Let's dive in.

2.1 LangChain: Building Modular AI Pipelines

LangChain is a powerful framework designed to help developers create modular AI pipelines that chain together various language model (LLM) calls, memory management components, and utilities into a cohesive workflow. In this guide, we will explore LangChain's core components, explain how they fit together, and walk through practical use cases with complete code examples.

Overview & Core Components

At its heart, LangChain is built around the idea of modularity. It breaks down an AI application into smaller, reusable pieces—each responsible for a specific part of the overall process. The main components include:

- **Chains:** These are sequences of calls to LLMs or other functions. A chain takes an input, processes it through one or more steps, and produces an output.
- **Prompts:** Templates that guide the behavior of the LLM by providing context and instructions. LangChain allows you to easily manage and format prompts.
- **Memory:** Modules that help maintain conversational context over time. Memory can store previous interactions to improve the relevance of responses.
- **Agents:** Higher-level constructs that decide which chain to execute based on user inputs and available tools. They can manage complex workflows by dynamically choosing actions.

These components can be combined in various ways to build applications ranging from simple chatbots to complex decision-support systems.

Practical Use Cases & Example Workflows

Use Case 1: Building a Conversational Assistant with Memory

Imagine you need to create a chatbot that not only answers questions but also remembers previous interactions. Using LangChain, you can set up a chain that incorporates memory for context retention.

Below is a complete example using LangChain to build a simple conversational assistant.

Step-by-Step Implementation

1. **Installation:**
   Make sure you have LangChain and OpenAI's Python package installed. You can install them via pip:

   ```bash
   pip install langchain openai
   ```

2. **Setting Up the Environment:**
   Import the necessary modules and set your OpenAI API key.

   ```python
   import os
   from langchain import OpenAI, ConversationChain
   from langchain.memory import ConversationBufferMemory

   # Set your OpenAI API key
   os.environ["OPENAI_API_KEY"] =
   "your_openai_api_key_here"
   ```

3. **Creating Memory and Conversation Chain:**
   Instantiate a memory module that will store the conversation history and use it within a conversation chain.

   ```python
   ```

```
# Initialize memory to store conversation context
memory =
ConversationBufferMemory(memory_key="chat_history",
return_messages=True)

# Create a conversation chain using OpenAI's model
conversation = ConversationChain(
    llm=OpenAI(temperature=0.7),
    memory=memory
)
```

4. **Interacting with the Assistant:**
   Now you can have a conversation with the assistant. Each input will update the conversation history, which the model uses to generate contextually relevant responses.

```python
python

# Simulate a conversation
user_input = "Hello, who won the world cup in 2018?"
response = conversation.predict(input=user_input)
print("Assistant:", response)

# Follow-up question that relies on previous context
user_input = "Can you tell me more about their
performance?"
response = conversation.predict(input=user_input)
print("Assistant:", response)
```

Explanation

- **Memory Integration:**
  The `ConversationBufferMemory` keeps a log of previous messages. When the assistant processes new inputs, it automatically includes this history, ensuring the conversation feels continuous.
- **Chain Functionality:**
  The `ConversationChain` ties together the LLM (OpenAI) and the memory, forming a modular pipeline. This separation of concerns makes it easy to swap components or add new ones later.

Use Case 2: Dynamic Content Generation with Chaining

Another practical example is an application that generates dynamic content such as marketing copy or blog posts. Here, you can chain multiple operations together—first summarizing key points and then expanding them into a full article.

Step-by-Step Implementation

1. **Installation:**
   Ensure LangChain and OpenAI packages are installed as shown previously.
2. **Defining Prompt Templates:**
   Create prompt templates for summarization and expansion tasks.

```python
from langchain.prompts import PromptTemplate

# Prompt template for summarizing input content
summary_prompt = PromptTemplate(
    input_variables=["content"],
    template="Summarize the following content in two sentences: {content}"
)

# Prompt template for expanding summary into a full article
expansion_prompt = PromptTemplate(
    input_variables=["summary"],
    template="Expand the following summary into a detailed blog post: {summary}"
)
```

3. **Chaining Operations:**
   Use LangChain's chaining capability to link the summarization and expansion processes.

```python
from langchain.chains import LLMChain

# Create chains for each step
summarization_chain =
LLMChain(llm=OpenAI(temperature=0.5),
prompt=summary_prompt)
expansion_chain = LLMChain(llm=OpenAI(temperature=0.8),
prompt=expansion_prompt)

# Combine the chains to create a full workflow
def generate_blog_post(content):
    summary = summarization_chain.run(content=content)
```

```
    full_article = expansion_chain.run(summary=summary)
    return full_article

# Test the workflow with sample content
sample_content = (
    "The tech industry has seen significant growth in
AI applications. "
    "Companies are leveraging AI to improve efficiency,
automate routine tasks, "
    "and provide enhanced customer experiences."
)
blog_post = generate_blog_post(sample_content)
print("Generated Blog Post:\n", blog_post)
```

Explanation

- **Prompt Templates:**
  These templates standardize the instructions for each LLM call. This
  ensures that each stage in the pipeline receives clear, structured input.
- **Chaining:**
  The output of the summarization chain becomes the input for the
  expansion chain. This sequential linking demonstrates the modular
  pipeline approach, where each step adds value to the final output.

Use Case 3: Multi-Step Reasoning and Action

LangChain can also support more complex workflows, such as
decision-support systems that require multi-step reasoning. Consider an
application where the system evaluates user requirements, fetches relevant
data, and then provides actionable recommendations.

Step-by-Step Implementation

1. **Setting Up the Scenario:**
   Define the various steps of the workflow through separate chains.

   ```python
   from langchain.chains import SequentialChain

   # Define a simple chain to evaluate user requirements
   evaluate_prompt = PromptTemplate(
       input_variables=["requirements"],
       template="Analyze the following requirements and
   list the key challenges: {requirements}"
   )
   ```

```
evaluation_chain =
LLMChain(llm=OpenAI(temperature=0.6),
prompt=evaluate_prompt)

# Define a chain to fetch data based on evaluation
fetch_data_prompt = PromptTemplate(
    input_variables=["challenges"],
    template="For each challenge listed, suggest a
potential data source that could help solve it:
{challenges}"
)
fetch_data_chain =
LLMChain(llm=OpenAI(temperature=0.7),
prompt=fetch_data_prompt)

# Combine into a sequential chain for multi-step
reasoning
sequential_workflow = SequentialChain(
    chains=[evaluation_chain, fetch_data_chain],
    input_variables=["requirements"],
    output_variables=["data_sources"]
)

# Execute the workflow
requirements = (
    "We need to improve our customer support system by
reducing response time and "
    "increasing accuracy in resolving common issues."
)
data_sources =
sequential_workflow.run(requirements=requirements)
print("Suggested Data Sources:\n", data_sources)
```

Explanation

- **SequentialChain:**
  This LangChain component allows you to create a multi-step pipeline where the output of one chain feeds directly into the next. It's perfect for scenarios requiring sequential reasoning.
- **Multi-Step Reasoning:**
  The first chain evaluates the problem, while the second chain uses that evaluation to suggest data sources, illustrating how LangChain supports dynamic and intelligent workflows.

Summary

LangChain's modular architecture empowers developers to build sophisticated AI pipelines by integrating multiple components—chains, prompts, memory, and agents—into a cohesive workflow. Whether you're designing a conversational assistant, generating dynamic content, or building a multi-step decision support system, LangChain provides the flexibility and power to transform ideas into functional applications.

By breaking down complex processes into smaller, manageable steps, LangChain not only enhances code reuse and maintainability but also accelerates the prototyping process. As you experiment with these concepts and explore the provided code examples, you'll discover that building modular AI pipelines becomes an intuitive and rewarding process. This approach not only streamlines development but also paves the way for scalable, production-grade AI systems.

Feel free to modify and extend these examples as you begin integrating LangChain into your own projects—each piece of the pipeline is designed to be interchangeable, letting you tailor the system precisely to your needs

2.2 CrewAI: Orchestrating Multi-Agent Systems

CrewAI is an innovative framework that makes it easy to design and orchestrate multi-agent systems by allowing you to define specific roles and manage task allocation among several agents. In this section, we explain how to set up a simple CrewAI workflow that integrates with LLMs and external tools. The example below demonstrates how to orchestrate two specialized agents—a sentiment analysis agent and a summarization agent—to work together on a single input. This hypothetical example uses a simplified API that represents common patterns in multi-agent orchestration.

Note: The following code example assumes that you have installed the CrewAI package (e.g., via `pip install crewai`) and that you have a valid OpenAI API key. The API shown here is illustrative and designed to demonstrate common design concepts in CrewAI.

Step-by-Step Example

1. Setting Up the Environment

Begin by importing the necessary modules. We assume CrewAI provides base classes such as `Agent` and an `Orchestrator` to coordinate agent interactions. We also import OpenAI for LLM calls.

```python
import os
import openai
from crewai import Agent, Orchestrator  # Hypothetical CrewAI
API

# Set your OpenAI API key (replace with your actual key)
os.environ["OPENAI_API_KEY"] = "your_openai_api_key_here"
```

2. Defining Specialized Agents

We define two agents:

- **SentimentAgent:** An agent that analyzes the sentiment of a given text.
- **SummarizationAgent:** An agent that summarizes the text.

Each agent inherits from a base `Agent` class and implements a `process` method that uses OpenAI's API to perform its function.

```python
class SentimentAgent(Agent):
    def __init__(self, name="SentimentAgent"):
        super().__init__(name)

    def process(self, text):
        # Use OpenAI's API to analyze sentiment
        response = openai.Completion.create(
            engine="text-davinci-003",
            prompt=f"Analyze the sentiment of this text and
respond with Positive, Negative, or Neutral: {text}",
            max_tokens=10,
            temperature=0.0,
        )
        sentiment = response.choices[0].text.strip()
        return sentiment
```

```
class SummarizationAgent(Agent):
    def __init__(self, name="SummarizationAgent"):
        super().__init__(name)

    def process(self, text):
        # Use OpenAI's API to generate a summary of the text
        response = openai.Completion.create(
            engine="text-davinci-003",
            prompt=f"Summarize the following text in two
sentences: {text}",
            max_tokens=100,
            temperature=0.5,
        )
        summary = response.choices[0].text.strip()
        return summary
```

Explanation:

- Each agent's `process` method makes a call to OpenAI's API with a clear prompt and parameters tailored to the task.
- The `SentimentAgent` returns a brief sentiment (e.g., "Positive"), while the `SummarizationAgent` provides a more detailed summary.

3. Orchestrating Agents with CrewAI

Next, we create an orchestrator instance to manage the agents. The orchestrator is responsible for coordinating the flow of tasks between agents.

```python
# Instantiate the specialized agents
sentiment_agent = SentimentAgent()
summarization_agent = SummarizationAgent()

# Create an orchestrator to coordinate the agents
orchestrator = Orchestrator(agents=[sentiment_agent,
summarization_agent])
```

4. Defining a Workflow

We define a function that uses the orchestrator to process an input text through both agents sequentially. This workflow demonstrates how one agent's output can be used independently or combined later.

```python
```

```
def orchestrate_workflow(input_text):
    print("Input Text:", input_text)

    # Step 1: Sentiment Analysis
    sentiment = sentiment_agent.process(input_text)
    print("Sentiment Analysis Result:", sentiment)

    # Step 2: Summarization
    summary = summarization_agent.process(input_text)
    print("Summarization Result:", summary)

    # Optionally, the orchestrator can manage further
integration or data passing
    # Here we simply return both outputs in a structured
format
    return {"sentiment": sentiment, "summary": summary}
```

Explanation:

- The workflow function prints the input text and then sequentially calls each agent's `process` method.
- Results from each agent are printed for clarity and returned as a dictionary, demonstrating how multiple outputs can be integrated.

5. Running the Workflow

Finally, we execute the workflow with a sample text. This complete example illustrates how CrewAI facilitates multi-agent orchestration in a clear and modular fashion.

```python
if __name__ == "__main__":
    sample_text = (
        "I had an amazing experience with the new product. "
        "The quality was superb and the customer service was
outstanding. "
        "I would definitely recommend it to my friends!"
    )
    results = orchestrate_workflow(sample_text)
    print("Final Orchestrated Results:", results)
```

Explanation:

- Running the script will process the sample text through both agents.

- The output shows the sentiment analysis and summary, offering a glimpse into how a multi-agent system can provide enriched insights from a single input.

Summary

This guide has walked through how to use CrewAI to orchestrate a multi-agent system by defining specialized agents for sentiment analysis and summarization, then coordinating their interaction using an orchestrator. By following these steps, you can build robust, modular pipelines that enable AI agents to work together seamlessly. This approach not only simplifies complex workflows but also enhances system flexibility and scalability.

Feel free to experiment with the code by adding more agents or integrating additional external tools to further customize your multi-agent system. As you develop your projects, consider how each agent's role can be fine-tuned, and how orchestration can be leveraged to create dynamic, context-aware AI systems that cater to your specific needs.

2.3 AutoGen: Creating Custom Conversational Agents

AutoGen is a robust framework designed by Microsoft for creating custom conversational agents using a multi-agent architecture. It provides developers with extensive customization options to tailor agents for specific tasks while enabling agents to work together to achieve complex goals. In this guide, you'll learn how to create a simple conversational agent that uses AutoGen's API to process user inputs, maintain conversational context, and produce meaningful responses.

Below is a comprehensive, step-by-step example, complete with detailed code snippets and explanations.

Step 1: Environment Setup

Before you begin, ensure you have the AutoGen package installed. (For this example, we assume AutoGen is available via pip.) Also, set your OpenAI API key as AutoGen uses OpenAI's models in the backend.

```bash
bash

pip install autogen openai
```

In your Python script, import the necessary modules and configure your API key:

```python
python

import os
from autogen import CustomAgent, ConversationSession  #
Hypothetical AutoGen API

# Set your OpenAI API key (replace with your actual key)
os.environ["OPENAI_API_KEY"] = "your_openai_api_key_here"
```

Explanation:

- The `CustomAgent` and `ConversationSession` classes (provided by AutoGen) will allow you to define a custom agent and maintain a conversational session.
- Setting the API key is crucial for authenticating requests to OpenAI's models.

Step 2: Defining Customization Functions

One of AutoGen's key strengths is its flexibility. You can define custom preprocessing and postprocessing functions to adjust how the agent handles input and output.

```python
python

def custom_preprocessing(text):
    """
    Preprocess the input text by stripping unnecessary
whitespace.
```

```
    Additional steps (like lowercasing or filtering) can be
added here.
    """
    return text.strip()

def custom_postprocessing(response):
    """
    Postprocess the agent's response to ensure it is well-
formatted.
    Additional modifications (like capitalization or
punctuation adjustments) can be added here.
    """
    return response.strip()
```

Explanation:

- The `custom_preprocessing` function cleans the user's input before it is sent to the language model.
- The `custom_postprocessing` function refines the raw response from the model before displaying it to the user.
- These functions help ensure consistency and improve the overall conversational experience.

Step 3: Creating the Custom Conversational Agent

Next, you will create a function to instantiate your custom conversational agent using AutoGen. This function sets up the agent, applies the customization functions, and creates a session to manage conversational context.

```python
python

def create_custom_conversational_agent():
    """
    Creates and returns a conversation session using
AutoGen's CustomAgent.
    The agent is configured with a specific model,
temperature, and custom processing functions.
    """
    # Instantiate the agent with a custom name and desired
model parameters
    agent = CustomAgent(name="CustomConversationalAgent",
model="gpt-4", temperature=0.7)

    # Set custom preprocessing and postprocessing functions
```

```python
    agent.set_preprocessing_function(custom_preprocessing)
    agent.set_postprocessing_function(custom_postprocessing)

    # Create a conversation session to maintain context
across interactions
    conversation = ConversationSession(agent=agent)

    return conversation
```

Explanation:

- The agent is initialized with a name, the model ("gpt-4"), and a temperature setting that controls response creativity.
- The customization functions are assigned to ensure that inputs and outputs are processed as needed.
- A `ConversationSession` is created to handle context retention, which is essential for maintaining coherent, ongoing conversations.

Step 4: Implementing the Conversation Loop

With the agent and session configured, implement a simple conversation loop that allows a user to interact with the agent through the command line.

```python
python

def main():
    # Create the conversational agent session
    conversation = create_custom_conversational_agent()

    print("Welcome to the custom conversational agent. Type
'exit' to quit.")

    # Continuous conversation loop
    while True:
        user_input = input("You: ")
        if user_input.lower() in ["exit", "quit"]:
            print("Exiting conversation. Goodbye!")
            break

        # Send the user input to the conversation session and
get a response
        response = conversation.send_message(user_input)
        print("Agent:", response)

if __name__ == '__main__':
```

```
    main()
```

Explanation:

- The `main` function initiates the conversation by creating the agent session.
- A loop continuously reads user input from the terminal. Typing "exit" or "quit" breaks the loop.
- The `send_message` method of the `ConversationSession` sends the input to the agent, which processes it (using your custom functions) and returns a response.
- The response is printed, completing one cycle of the conversation.

Full Code Example

Below is the complete, functional code for creating a custom conversational agent with AutoGen:

```python
python

import os
from autogen import CustomAgent, ConversationSession  #
Hypothetical AutoGen API

# Set your OpenAI API key (replace with your actual key)
os.environ["OPENAI_API_KEY"] = "your_openai_api_key_here"

def custom_preprocessing(text):
    """
    Preprocess the input text by stripping unnecessary
whitespace.
    Additional processing steps can be added as needed.
    """
    return text.strip()

def custom_postprocessing(response):
    """
    Postprocess the agent's response to ensure it is well-
formatted.
    Additional modifications can be applied here.
    """
    return response.strip()

def create_custom_conversational_agent():
    """
```

```
        Creates and returns a conversation session using
AutoGen's CustomAgent.
        The agent is configured with a specific model,
temperature, and custom processing functions.
        """
        # Instantiate the agent with custom parameters
        agent = CustomAgent(name="CustomConversationalAgent",
model="gpt-4", temperature=0.7)

        # Assign custom preprocessing and postprocessing
functions
        agent.set_preprocessing_function(custom_preprocessing)
        agent.set_postprocessing_function(custom_postprocessing)

        # Create a conversation session to maintain context
        conversation = ConversationSession(agent=agent)

        return conversation

def main():
        # Create the conversational agent session
        conversation = create_custom_conversational_agent()

        print("Welcome to the custom conversational agent. Type
'exit' to quit.")

        # Conversation loop for continuous interaction
        while True:
            user_input = input("You: ")
            if user_input.lower() in ["exit", "quit"]:
                print("Exiting conversation. Goodbye!")
                break

            # Process the input and get a response from the agent
            response = conversation.send_message(user_input)
            print("Agent:", response)

if __name__ == '__main__':
        main()
```

This guide demonstrated how to create a custom conversational agent using AutoGen. We started by setting up the environment and defining custom processing functions to ensure high-quality interactions. Then, we built the agent, established a conversation session, and implemented a loop to handle continuous user input.

The modular design of AutoGen makes it simple to extend and customize. You can easily add more sophisticated preprocessing steps, integrate additional tools, or even develop multi-agent architectures that work together for more complex tasks. As you experiment with this example, consider how you might refine the agent's behavior to suit specific use cases—whether that's enhancing customer support, streamlining internal communications, or any other application where intelligent conversation can make a difference.

By mastering these concepts and practical implementations, you'll be well-prepared to build advanced conversational agents that are both robust and adaptable. Enjoy exploring the possibilities with AutoGen, and use this foundation to power your next innovative project in AI.

2.4 LlamaIndex: Data Integration and Retrieval

LlamaIndex is a versatile library designed to bridge the gap between large language models (LLMs) and external data sources. By creating an index over your data—whether it comes from text files, PDFs, or web pages—you can empower your AI agents to retrieve and reason over large datasets quickly. This guide walks you through a practical example of how to use LlamaIndex for data integration and retrieval, complete with step-by-step explanations and fully functional code examples.

Step 1: Installation and Setup

Before using LlamaIndex, you must install the library. You can do this via pip:

```bash

pip install llama-index
```

Explanation:
This command installs the latest version of LlamaIndex, making it available for your Python projects.

Step 2: Loading External Data

LlamaIndex can ingest data from various sources. In this example, we'll use a simple text dataset stored in a directory. The library provides utility classes such as `SimpleDirectoryReader` to help load documents.

```python
from llama_index import SimpleDirectoryReader

# Load all text files from the 'data' directory
documents = SimpleDirectoryReader('data').load_data()

# Print out the number of documents loaded for verification
print(f"Loaded {len(documents)} documents.")
```

Explanation:

- **SimpleDirectoryReader:** This class reads all text files in the specified directory.
- **load_data():** This method returns a list of document objects that LlamaIndex can process further.
- Printing the number of documents gives you quick feedback that your data is correctly loaded.

Step 3: Building the Index

With your documents loaded, the next step is to build an index. LlamaIndex offers a vector store index that maps document embeddings to the original content. This index allows LLMs to quickly search and retrieve relevant sections of your data.

```python
from llama_index import GPTVectorStoreIndex

# Create a vector store index from the loaded documents
index = GPTVectorStoreIndex.from_documents(documents)

# Optional: Save the index for later use (serialization)
index.save_to_disk('index.json')
```

Explanation:

- **GPTVectorStoreIndex:** This class creates an index using embeddings generated from your documents.
- **from_documents(documents):** This class method processes the documents and constructs an index that can be queried later.
- Saving the index to disk is useful if you need to reuse it without rebuilding from scratch.

Step 4: Querying the Index

Once the index is built, you can query it to retrieve information. This is where LLMs come into play—they use the index to understand the context of your query and fetch the most relevant content.

```python
python

# Define a query to ask about the content of your documents
query = "What are the main themes discussed in these
documents?"

# Query the index and get a response
response = index.query(query)

# Print the response from the LLM
print("Query Response:")
print(response)
```

Explanation:

- **query(query):** This method takes a natural language query and uses the index to fetch and process the most relevant parts of your documents.
- The response is generated by an LLM that has been augmented with the indexed data, meaning it can provide answers grounded in your external data.

Full Code Example

Below is the complete code, combining all the steps into a cohesive workflow:

```python

import os
from llama_index import SimpleDirectoryReader,
GPTVectorStoreIndex

# Ensure your working directory contains a folder named
'data' with text files
# Step 1: Load documents from the 'data' directory
documents = SimpleDirectoryReader('data').load_data()
print(f"Loaded {len(documents)} documents.")

# Step 2: Build an index from the documents
index = GPTVectorStoreIndex.from_documents(documents)
# Save the index for later reuse (optional)
index.save_to_disk('index.json')

# Step 3: Query the index with a natural language query
query = "What are the main themes discussed in these
documents?"
response = index.query(query)

# Output the query response
print("Query Response:")
print(response)
```

Explanation of the Full Example:

- **Loading Data:** The code starts by reading all text files from a directory named `data`.
- **Building the Index:** It then builds a vector store index from these documents, which is the foundation for efficient retrieval.
- **Querying:** Finally, the code queries the index using a natural language prompt, with the resulting response printed to the console.

Practical Implementation Considerations

- **Data Quality:** Ensure that the documents in your data directory are well-structured and clean. Poor-quality data can lead to less relevant query responses.
- **Index Maintenance:** For dynamic datasets, consider updating the index regularly or implementing a mechanism to automatically rebuild the index as new documents are added.

- **Query Customization:** You can fine-tune the query behavior by adjusting parameters such as the LLM's temperature or by refining your query prompts.

LlamaIndex empowers developers to integrate external data seamlessly into AI-driven applications. By converting raw documents into a searchable index, it enables LLMs to provide precise and contextually rich responses. This step-by-step guide has shown you how to set up, build, and query an index using LlamaIndex, laying the groundwork for more sophisticated applications such as knowledge bases, research assistants, and dynamic content generators.

As you expand your projects, consider exploring additional features of LlamaIndex, such as custom embeddings, advanced query options, and integration with other data sources, to further enhance your AI agent's capabilities.

2.5 GPT Engineer: Automating Code Generation and Debugging

GPT Engineer is an innovative tool designed to bridge the gap between natural language instructions and executable code. By leveraging advanced language models, it can translate your high-level descriptions into functional code and assist in debugging and refining that code. In this guide, you will learn how to set up GPT Engineer, generate code based on a plain language prompt, and apply debugging strategies to refine the output. The step-by-step process below includes complete, functional code examples to illustrate practical implementations.

Overview & Key Features

GPT Engineer automates two major parts of the software development process:

- **Code Generation:** It transforms natural language descriptions into working code. This allows you to describe a desired functionality in plain English and receive a complete code snippet that implements that functionality.
- **Debugging and Refinement:** If the generated code encounters errors or doesn't meet your expectations, GPT Engineer can analyze error messages or problematic behavior and suggest corrections, streamlining the debugging process.

These capabilities not only speed up development but also lower the barrier for non-expert programmers to build complex systems.

Step-by-Step Implementation

Step 1: Installation and Environment Setup

Assume GPT Engineer is available as a Python package. Start by installing it along with OpenAI's Python package (which powers the underlying language model):

```bash
pip install gpt-engineer openai
```

Next, set your OpenAI API key in your environment. This key is required for authenticating API calls to generate and refine code.

```python
import os

# Replace with your actual OpenAI API key
os.environ["OPENAI_API_KEY"] = "your_openai_api_key_here"
```

Explanation:

- The installation command ensures you have both GPT Engineer and the necessary OpenAI library.
- Setting the API key as an environment variable allows the library to access OpenAI's services securely.

Step 2: Generating Code from Natural Language

GPT Engineer exposes functions to convert plain language prompts into code. In this example, we will generate a Python function that takes a list of numbers and returns the sum of all even numbers.

```python
from gpt_engineer import generate_code  # Hypothetical import
from GPT Engineer

# Define your natural language prompt
prompt = "Write a Python function called sum_even that takes
a list of numbers and returns the sum of all even numbers."

# Generate code based on the prompt
generated_code = generate_code(prompt)

print("Generated Code:\n")
print(generated_code)
```

Explanation:

- The `generate_code` function sends the prompt to GPT Engineer, which interacts with the language model to produce the desired code.
- The printed output should be a complete Python function that implements the requested functionality.

Step 3: Debugging and Refinement

Sometimes the initially generated code might contain errors or require improvements. GPT Engineer can help refine the code by analyzing error messages and suggesting corrections. For example, if you run the generated code and encounter a `NameError`, you can pass this error message to a debugging function.

```python
from gpt_engineer import debug_code  # Hypothetical import
from GPT Engineer
```

```python
# Simulate an error encountered during execution
error_message = "NameError: name 'sum_even' is not defined"

# Pass the generated code and error message to refine the
code
refined_code = debug_code(generated_code, error_message)

print("Refined Code:\n")
print(refined_code)
```

Explanation:

- The `debug_code` function takes the initial code and an error message, then uses the language model to generate a refined version.
- This process mimics a pair programming scenario where the tool acts as an intelligent assistant, guiding you to a corrected implementation.

Step 4: Combining Code Generation and Debugging in a Sample Project

To see how these pieces work together, consider the following full example that integrates both code generation and debugging.

```python
python

import os
from gpt_engineer import generate_code, debug_code   #
Hypothetical GPT Engineer API

# Set your OpenAI API key
os.environ["OPENAI_API_KEY"] = "your_openai_api_key_here"

def create_sum_even_function():
    """
    Generates a Python function that sums even numbers from a
list.
    Returns the generated code as a string.
    """
    prompt = (
        "Write a Python function called sum_even that takes a
list of numbers "
        "and returns the sum of all even numbers."
    )
    code = generate_code(prompt)
    return code
```

```
def refine_code_if_needed(code):
    """
    Simulates running the generated code and refines it if an
error is encountered.
    In this example, we simulate a NameError.
    """
    # Simulate an error message (in a real scenario, you
would capture this from execution)
    error_message = "NameError: name 'sum_even' is not
defined"
    # Refine the code based on the error message
    refined = debug_code(code, error_message)
    return refined

def main():
    # Step 1: Generate the initial code
    print("Generating code for sum_even function...")
    initial_code = create_sum_even_function()
    print("Initial Generated Code:\n")
    print(initial_code)

    # Step 2: Simulate debugging and refining the code
    print("\nRefining the generated code based on simulated
error feedback...")
    final_code = refine_code_if_needed(initial_code)
    print("Final Refined Code:\n")
    print(final_code)

if __name__ == "__main__":
    main()
```

Explanation:

- **create_sum_even_function()**: Uses a natural language prompt to generate code for a specific function.
- **refine_code_if_needed()**: Simulates error handling by passing a predefined error message to the debugging function.
- **main()**: Orchestrates the workflow by first generating the code and then refining it if necessary, finally printing out both versions.

GPT Engineer streamlines the process of converting natural language requirements into executable code and provides an intelligent mechanism for debugging and refinement. By following the steps outlined in this guide, you can leverage GPT Engineer to automate parts of your coding workflow, reducing manual effort and accelerating development.

This comprehensive approach—starting from a plain language description to generating and refining code—illustrates how GPT Engineer can act as your AI-powered pair programmer. As you experiment with the tool, you may extend these examples by integrating more complex prompts, handling real-time error capture, and developing multi-functional codebases. The modular design of GPT Engineer makes it adaptable to a wide range of programming tasks, empowering you to focus on innovation while the tool handles the boilerplate work.

2.6 Semantic Kernel: Integrating LLMs with Intelligent Workflows

Semantic Kernel is a framework developed by Microsoft to help you integrate large language models (LLMs) directly into intelligent workflows. It offers built-in memory management, prompt chaining, and composable modules that let you design flexible, context-aware applications. In this guide, we'll walk through setting up Semantic Kernel in Python, integrating an LLM service, and building a simple workflow that uses memory and prompt templates.

Step 1: Installation and Environment Setup

First, ensure that you have Semantic Kernel installed. If it's available on PyPI, you can install it via pip. (Replace the package name with the correct one if necessary.)

```bash
pip install semantic-kernel
```

Next, set up your environment by importing the necessary modules and configuring your LLM service (in this case, we'll use OpenAI's GPT-4).

```python
```

```
import os
import semantic_kernel as sk
from semantic_kernel.connectors.llm.openai import
OpenAITextCompletion

# Set your OpenAI API key for authentication
os.environ["OPENAI_API_KEY"] = "your_openai_api_key_here"
```

Explanation:

- The `semantic_kernel` package provides the core framework.
- The `OpenAITextCompletion` connector lets you integrate OpenAI's models into your workflow.

Step 2: Initializing the Kernel and LLM Service

Semantic Kernel uses a central "kernel" object to manage skills, memory, and LLM interactions. Create an instance of the kernel and add an LLM service.

```python
# Initialize the Semantic Kernel instance
kernel = sk.Kernel()

# Create an OpenAI LLM service instance with the desired
model and temperature
llm_service = OpenAITextCompletion(
    api_key=os.environ["OPENAI_API_KEY"],
    model="gpt-4",
    temperature=0.7
)

# Add the LLM service to the kernel with an identifier
kernel.add_text_completion_service("openai", llm_service)
```

Explanation:

- The kernel acts as the orchestrator for your intelligent workflow.
- Adding the LLM service under a name (here, "openai") allows you to refer to it in later operations.

Step 3: Incorporating Built-in Memory

One of Semantic Kernel's key features is its ability to maintain context through memory. The memory component enables the system to store past interactions and reference them in future tasks. Here, we instantiate a simple memory store and connect it to the kernel.

```python
# Initialize a memory store (assume semantic_kernel provides
a basic Memory class)
memory = sk.Memory()

# Attach the memory to the kernel so that it automatically
retains context
kernel.set_memory(memory)
```

Explanation:

- Memory is essential for creating context-aware workflows.
- In a real-world scenario, this memory could be persistent (saving history between sessions) or temporary (for the current conversation).

Step 4: Creating a Prompt Template for an Intelligent Workflow

Next, we'll create a prompt template. In this example, we define a task to summarize a block of text. The prompt template lets you define placeholders (such as {text}) that will be dynamically replaced with input data.

```python
# Define a prompt template with a placeholder for input text
prompt_template = """
You are a knowledgeable assistant. Please summarize the
following text in one concise paragraph:

{text}

Summary:
"""

# Create a Semantic Kernel PromptTemplate instance
template = sk.PromptTemplate(prompt_template,
input_variables=["text"])
```

Explanation:

- The prompt template is structured to provide clear instructions to the LLM.
- Placeholders (e.g., `{text}`) are replaced with actual content when the template is rendered.

Step 5: Building a Workflow Function

With the kernel, LLM service, memory, and prompt template in place, you can now build a function that executes an intelligent workflow. This function will take a block of text as input, use the prompt template to generate a summary, and automatically incorporate any existing context from memory.

```python
def generate_summary(input_text: str) -> str:
    """
    Generates a summary of the input text using Semantic
Kernel.

    Args:
        input_text (str): The text to be summarized.

    Returns:
        str: A concise summary generated by the LLM.
    """
    # Render the prompt template with the given input text
    prompt = template.render({"text": input_text})

    # Use the kernel to complete the prompt with the LLM
service
    # The complete() method sends the prompt to the specified
service ("openai")
    result = kernel.complete("openai", prompt)

    # Optionally, the kernel's memory may update with this
interaction
    return result.strip()
```

Explanation:

- The function `generate_summary` renders the prompt using the provided input.

- It calls `kernel.complete()`, specifying the LLM service by its identifier ("openai"), to generate a response.
- The result is trimmed and returned as a summary.

Step 6: Testing the Intelligent Workflow

Now, let's put everything together by running the workflow with a sample text. This demonstrates how Semantic Kernel integrates LLMs, memory, and prompt templates into a seamless intelligent workflow.

```python
if __name__ == "__main__":
    # Sample text to summarize
    sample_text = (
        "Semantic Kernel is a framework that allows
developers to integrate large language models "
        "into their applications in a modular and context-
aware manner. It provides built-in memory "
        "and chaining capabilities that enable the
development of intelligent workflows which learn "
        "and adapt over time."
    )

    # Generate a summary using the workflow
    summary = generate_summary(sample_text)

    print("Input Text:")
    print(sample_text)
    print("\nGenerated Summary:")
    print(summary)
```

Explanation:

- The main block tests the workflow by summarizing a sample text.
- The output shows both the original text and the generated summary, illustrating how Semantic Kernel processes the input and produces a concise output.

Semantic Kernel simplifies the integration of LLMs into intelligent workflows by offering a modular framework with built-in memory, prompt templating, and flexible orchestration. Through this step-by-step guide, you have seen how to set up the kernel, configure an LLM service, incorporate memory, create prompt templates, and build a complete workflow that generates a summary.

This example is a starting point. As you become more comfortable with Semantic Kernel, you can extend this framework to build more complex workflows—such as multi-step reasoning processes, interactive chatbots, or systems that combine multiple skills in a coordinated manner. The power of Semantic Kernel lies in its flexibility, allowing you to experiment, iterate, and ultimately build robust applications that respond intelligently to real-world scenarios.

2.7 SuperAGI: Deploying Autonomous Agents at Scale

SuperAGI is an open-source framework designed to deploy autonomous agents at scale. It focuses on creating production-grade AI agents that can handle complex, multi-step tasks while operating in real-world environments. SuperAGI combines advanced natural language processing with orchestration tools to manage agents, making it possible to scale your AI workflows efficiently. This guide will walk you through setting up SuperAGI, configuring an agent, and orchestrating tasks using an example codebase.

Step 1: Installation and Environment Setup

Before you can use SuperAGI, you need to install the package and set up your development environment. Assuming SuperAGI is available on PyPI, install it with:

```bash
pip install superagi
```

Next, import the necessary modules and set up your API key if you are using a backend LLM service (such as OpenAI's GPT-4).

```python
import os
```

```
from superagi.agent import SuperAgent
from superagi.orchestrator import AgentOrchestrator

# Set your OpenAI API key (replace with your actual key)
os.environ["OPENAI_API_KEY"] = "your_openai_api_key_here"
```

Explanation:

- The installation command fetches the latest SuperAGI package.
- We import the key components: `SuperAgent` for creating individual agents and `AgentOrchestrator` for managing multiple agents.
- The API key is necessary to authenticate calls to the underlying language model.

Step 2: Creating and Configuring a SuperAGI Agent

SuperAGI allows you to instantiate agents with customizable parameters. In this example, we'll create an agent named "ProductionAgent" that leverages GPT-4 with a specified temperature to control its creativity.

```python
python

# Instantiate a SuperAGI agent with specific parameters
agent = SuperAgent(
    name="ProductionAgent",
    model="gpt-4",          # Specify the model to use
    temperature=0.7         # Adjust temperature for creativity
vs. determinism
)
```

Explanation:

- The `SuperAgent` class encapsulates the logic for an autonomous agent.
- Parameters such as `name`, `model`, and `temperature` are set to tailor the agent's behavior.

Step 3: Orchestrating Multiple Agents

For production systems, you may need to deploy multiple agents that collaborate to complete complex tasks. SuperAGI's `AgentOrchestrator` enables you to register agents and manage task allocation between them. In this example, we create an orchestrator and register our single agent. In a more complex scenario, you can add multiple specialized agents.

```python
# Initialize an orchestrator to manage agents
orchestrator = AgentOrchestrator()

# Register the agent with the orchestrator
orchestrator.register_agent(agent)
```

Explanation:

- The orchestrator coordinates how agents receive tasks and interact.
- Registering an agent with the orchestrator allows it to be managed alongside other agents in a scalable setup.

Step 4: Defining an Autonomous Task Workflow

With the agent and orchestrator in place, you can define a workflow function that takes a high-level task description, passes it to the orchestrator, and returns the result. Here, we simulate a task where the agent is asked to analyze sales data and generate key insights.

```python
def run_autonomous_task(input_task: str) -> str:
    """
    Executes an autonomous task using the registered agent(s)
via the orchestrator.

    Args:
        input_task (str): A high-level task description.

    Returns:
        str: The result produced by the agent.
    """
```

```
    # The orchestrator directs the input task to the
appropriate agent
    result = orchestrator.execute(input_task)
    return result.strip()
```

Explanation:

- The function `run_autonomous_task` takes a plain language task as input.
- The orchestrator's `execute` method sends the task to the registered agent. The agent processes the task autonomously and returns a result.
- Trimming the result ensures that any extraneous whitespace is removed.

Step 5: Running the Complete Workflow

Finally, integrate the previous steps into a main function to execute the workflow. This example demonstrates the end-to-end process of deploying a task through SuperAGI.

```python
python

if __name__ == "__main__":
    # Define a sample task for the agent
    task = "Analyze our recent sales data and provide a
summary of key insights."

    print("Running autonomous task with SuperAGI...")

    # Run the task through the orchestrator
    output = run_autonomous_task(task)

    # Output the result
    print("Task Output:")
    print(output)
```

Explanation:

- The main block defines a high-level task and sends it through the `run_autonomous_task` function.
- The agent, managed by the orchestrator, processes the task and outputs its result.

- This integration exemplifies how SuperAGI can deploy autonomous agents in a production-like environment.

SuperAGI offers a powerful solution for deploying autonomous AI agents at scale. By combining robust agent creation with effective orchestration, it enables you to build systems that handle complex tasks across multiple domains. This guide has demonstrated how to set up your environment, create a SuperAGI agent, register it with an orchestrator, and execute an autonomous task workflow.

The modularity of SuperAGI means that you can expand this basic framework to include multiple specialized agents, implement error handling, and add monitoring to suit your production needs. Experiment with different models, tweak parameters like temperature, and explore advanced orchestration strategies to build resilient, scalable AI systems.

2.8 LangFlow: Prototyping Agent Workflows Visually

LangFlow provides a graphical, node-based interface to design and prototype AI agent workflows visually. It allows developers to drag and drop components (or nodes), configure them with parameters, and connect them to form complete pipelines that integrate language models, data processing, and other operations. In this guide, you will learn how to start LangFlow, design a simple workflow using its GUI, export the workflow as a JSON configuration, and then load and execute that configuration in Python using LangChain components.

Step 1: Installing and Launching LangFlow

First, install LangFlow via pip. (Make sure you have Python 3.7+ installed.) Then, start the LangFlow server, which opens a web interface in your browser.

```bash
pip install langflow
```

Explanation:

- The `pip install langflow` command installs the latest version of LangFlow.
- Running `langflow` starts a local server (typically on port 8000), and your default browser will open the visual interface where you can build workflows by dragging and dropping nodes.

Step 2: Designing Your Workflow in the LangFlow GUI

Once the GUI is open, you'll see a canvas where you can add nodes representing different actions. For example, you might create a workflow that summarizes text by combining a prompt node with an LLM node.

1. **Add a Prompt Node:**
   o Drag a "Prompt" node onto the canvas.
   o Configure its text to instruct the LLM, e.g., "Summarize the following text:"
2. **Add an LLM Node:**
   o Drag an "LLM" node (which uses a language model such as GPT-4) onto the canvas.
   o Set parameters like temperature (e.g., 0.7) and model name (e.g., "gpt-4").
3. **Connect the Nodes:**
   o Draw an edge from the Prompt node to the LLM node. This edge indicates that the output from the prompt will be passed to the LLM for processing.
4. **Export the Workflow:**
   o Once satisfied with the configuration, use the export function (often available via a button or menu option) to save the workflow as a JSON file (e.g., `workflow.json`).

Explanation:
Using the LangFlow interface, you can visually assemble the components of your AI pipeline. This method is particularly useful for brainstorming and rapid prototyping since it lowers the barrier to creating complex workflows without writing code manually.

Step 3: Loading and Executing the Workflow in Python

After exporting your workflow configuration, you can integrate it with your Python code. The exported JSON contains the details of each node and how they are connected. In this example, we assume a simple workflow with two nodes—a prompt node and an LLM node. We then build a corresponding LangChain pipeline.

Sample JSON Workflow

Assume your exported `workflow.json` looks like this:

```json
{
  "nodes": [
    {
      "id": "node1",
      "type": "Prompt",
      "prompt": "Summarize the following text:"
    },
    {
      "id": "node2",
      "type": "LLM",
      "model": "gpt-4",
      "temperature": 0.7
    }
  ],
  "edges": [
    {
      "from": "node1",
      "to": "node2"
    }
  ]
}
```

Explanation:
This JSON configuration defines two nodes:

- The first node is a Prompt node that provides a template.
- The second node is an LLM node configured to use GPT-4 with a temperature of 0.7. The edge indicates that the output of the Prompt node feeds into the LLM node.

Step 3.1: Writing Code to Build the Workflow

Below is a complete Python example that loads the JSON configuration, builds a LangChain pipeline, and executes it with an input string.

```python
python

import json
from langchain.chains import LLMChain, SimpleSequentialChain
from langchain.prompts import PromptTemplate
from langchain.llms import OpenAI

# Ensure your OpenAI API key is set in your environment
import os
os.environ["OPENAI_API_KEY"] = "your_openai_api_key_here"

def load_workflow_config(file_path: str) -> dict:
    """
    Loads the workflow configuration from a JSON file.

    Args:
        file_path (str): The path to the JSON configuration
file.

    Returns:
        dict: The workflow configuration.
    """
    with open(file_path, "r") as file:
        config = json.load(file)
    return config

def build_chain_from_config(config: dict) ->
SimpleSequentialChain:
    """
    Builds a simple sequential chain from the workflow
configuration.
    Assumes a two-node workflow: a Prompt node and an LLM
node.

    Args:
        config (dict): The workflow configuration.

    Returns:
        SimpleSequentialChain: The constructed LangChain
pipeline.
    """
    # Extract prompt text from the first node
    prompt_text = config["nodes"][0]["prompt"]
```

```python
    # Create a prompt template that expects an input variable
'text'
    prompt_template = PromptTemplate(
        input_variables=["text"],
        template=f"{prompt_text} {{text}}"
    )

    # Extract model configuration from the second node
    llm_config = config["nodes"][1]
    model_name = llm_config.get("model", "gpt-4")
    temperature = llm_config.get("temperature", 0.7)

    # Initialize the OpenAI LLM with the extracted parameters
    llm = OpenAI(temperature=temperature,
model_name=model_name)

    # Create an LLMChain that combines the prompt template
with the LLM
    chain = LLMChain(llm=llm, prompt=prompt_template,
verbose=True)

    # Wrap the chain in a SimpleSequentialChain (useful for
multi-step workflows)
    sequential_chain = SimpleSequentialChain(chains=[chain],
verbose=True)

    return sequential_chain

def main():
    # Load the workflow configuration exported from LangFlow
    config = load_workflow_config("workflow.json")
    print("Workflow configuration loaded successfully.")

    # Build the chain from the configuration
    chain = build_chain_from_config(config)
    print("LangChain pipeline built successfully.")

    # Define an input text to process through the workflow
    input_text = "Artificial intelligence is transforming
industries by automating complex tasks."

    # Execute the chain with the input text
    result = chain.run(input_text)
    print("Workflow Result:")
    print(result)

if __name__ == "__main__":
    main()
```

Detailed Explanation:

1. **Loading the Configuration:**
   The `load_workflow_config` function reads the exported JSON file (`workflow.json`) and parses it into a Python dictionary.
2. **Building the Chain:**
   - The function `build_chain_from_config` extracts details from the JSON.
   - It creates a `PromptTemplate` using the prompt from the first node.
   - It then reads the LLM configuration (model and temperature) from the second node and initializes the corresponding OpenAI LLM instance.
   - An `LLMChain` is created by combining the prompt template and the LLM, and finally wrapped in a `SimpleSequentialChain` to support multi-step workflows if needed.
3. **Executing the Workflow:**
   - In the `main` function, after loading and building the chain, an input text is processed through the chain.
   - The result, which is the summary or transformation produced by the LLM, is printed out.

LangFlow's visual interface empowers developers to design agent workflows without writing code manually, while its ability to export configurations as JSON allows seamless integration with Python-based tools like LangChain. This guide has provided a comprehensive walkthrough—from installing and launching LangFlow, designing a workflow visually, to loading the configuration and executing it with a fully functional Python script.

As you experiment with LangFlow, consider how you can extend these examples. You might add additional nodes for tasks like sentiment analysis, data retrieval, or even conditional branching. The modular nature of LangFlow and LangChain allows you to iterate quickly and build increasingly sophisticated AI pipelines that can address a wide range of real-world problems.

By integrating a visual prototyping tool with robust code execution frameworks, you have a powerful toolkit at your disposal—one that makes designing, testing, and scaling intelligent agent workflows both efficient and accessible. Enjoy exploring the possibilities and pushing the boundaries of what your AI systems can achieve.

2.9 AgentGPT: Browser-Based Agent Configuration and Deployment

AgentGPT is a platform that simplifies the configuration and deployment of autonomous AI agents via a browser-based interface. It allows you to set up, manage, and customize your agents without writing extensive backend code. In this guide, you'll learn how to create a simple web application that uses AgentGPT functionality to process user prompts and return AI-generated responses. We'll use Flask as our web framework to build a complete, functional example.

Step 1: Installing and Setting Up the Environment

Before you begin, install the required packages. For this example, we'll need Flask and OpenAI's Python package. Run the following command in your terminal:

```bash
bash

pip install flask openai
```

Explanation:

- **Flask** provides a lightweight web server to host our browser-based interface.
- **OpenAI** allows us to call language models (which underlie AgentGPT's functionality) to generate responses.

Set up your environment by creating a new Python script (for example, `app.py`) and configuring your API key:

```python
python

import os
from flask import Flask, render_template, request, jsonify
import openai
```

```
# Set your OpenAI API key (replace with your actual key)
os.environ["OPENAI_API_KEY"] = "your_openai_api_key_here"
openai.api_key = os.environ["OPENAI_API_KEY"]

# Initialize the Flask application
app = Flask(__name__)
```

Explanation:
This code imports necessary modules, sets your OpenAI API key (essential for authentication), and initializes the Flask application.

Step 2: Implementing AgentGPT Functionality

For our purposes, we'll simulate AgentGPT functionality by creating a helper function that sends user input to the OpenAI API and retrieves a response. In a full AgentGPT deployment, you might have additional layers of configuration and management, but this example demonstrates the core idea.

```python
python

def agentgpt_response(prompt):
    """
    Processes the given prompt using OpenAI's language model
and returns the generated response.

    Args:
        prompt (str): The input text prompt from the user.

    Returns:
        str: The AI-generated response.
    """
    response = openai.Completion.create(
        engine="text-davinci-003",  # Replace with your
preferred model (e.g., "gpt-4" if available)
        prompt=prompt,
        max_tokens=150,
        temperature=0.7,
    )
    return response.choices[0].text.strip()
```

Explanation:

- **agentgpt_response:** This function takes a prompt, sends it to the OpenAI API, and returns the generated text.
- Parameters like `max_tokens` and `temperature` control the length and creativity of the response.

Step 3: Creating a Browser-Based Interface

We now set up our Flask routes to serve an HTML page where users can interact with the agent. Create an HTML template (e.g., in a folder named `templates`) called `index.html`:

File: templates/index.html

```html
html

<!doctype html>
<html lang="en">
<head>
  <meta charset="utf-8">
  <title>AgentGPT Deployment</title>
  <script src="https://code.jquery.com/jquery-
3.6.0.min.js"></script>
  <style>
    body { font-family: Arial, sans-serif; margin: 2em; }
    textarea { width: 100%; padding: 0.5em; }
    button { padding: 0.5em 1em; font-size: 1em; }
    #response { margin-top: 1em; background-color: #f0f0f0;
padding: 1em; border-radius: 5px; }
  </style>
</head>
<body>
  <h1>AgentGPT: Browser-Based Agent Configuration</h1>
  <form id="agent-form">
    <textarea id="user_input" name="user_input" rows="4"
placeholder="Enter your prompt here..."></textarea><br>
    <button type="submit">Submit</button>
  </form>
  <div id="response">
    <h2>Agent Response:</h2>
    <p id="result_text"></p>
  </div>

  <script>
    $('#agent-form').on('submit', function(event) {
      event.preventDefault();
      $.ajax({
```

```
      type: 'POST',
      url: '/process',
      data: $(this).serialize(),
      success: function(data) {
        $('#result_text').text(data.result);
      }
    });
  });
</script>
</body>
</html>
```

Explanation:

- The HTML file creates a simple user interface with a text area for input and a section to display the agent's response.
- jQuery is used to send the form data asynchronously to our backend endpoint, ensuring the page doesn't reload on submission.

Step 4: Implementing the Backend Route

Now, add a route in your app.py that handles the form submission, calls the agentgpt_response function, and returns the result as JSON.

```python
python

@app.route('/')
def index():
    """
    Renders the main page for the AgentGPT interface.
    """
    return render_template('index.html')

@app.route('/process', methods=['POST'])
def process():
    """
    Processes the user's input, generates a response using
the AgentGPT function, and returns the result.
    """
    user_input = request.form.get('user_input', '')
    result = agentgpt_response(user_input)
    return jsonify({'result': result})
```

Explanation:

- **index route:** Renders the HTML interface.
- **process route:** Retrieves user input from the form, processes it with `agentgpt_response`, and sends back the generated result as JSON.

Step 5: Running the Application

Finally, set up the main block to run your Flask application.

```python
if __name__ == '__main__':
    # Run the Flask application in debug mode
    app.run(debug=True)
```

Explanation:

- Running the application in debug mode is helpful during development. In a production environment, you'd disable debug mode and possibly use a production server like Gunicorn.

Complete Code Example

Below is the complete code for `app.py`:

```python
import os
from flask import Flask, render_template, request, jsonify
import openai

# Set your OpenAI API key (replace with your actual key)
os.environ["OPENAI_API_KEY"] = "your_openai_api_key_here"
openai.api_key = os.environ["OPENAI_API_KEY"]

# Initialize the Flask application
app = Flask(__name__)

def agentgpt_response(prompt):
    """
    Processes the given prompt using OpenAI's language model
and returns the generated response.
```

```
    Args:
        prompt (str): The input text prompt from the user.

    Returns:
        str: The AI-generated response.
    """
    response = openai.Completion.create(
        engine="text-davinci-003",  # Replace with "gpt-4" if
available
        prompt=prompt,
        max_tokens=150,
        temperature=0.7,
    )
    return response.choices[0].text.strip()

@app.route('/')
def index():
    """
    Renders the main page for the AgentGPT interface.
    """
    return render_template('index.html')

@app.route('/process', methods=['POST'])
def process():
    """
    Processes the user's input, generates a response using
the AgentGPT function, and returns the result.
    """
    user_input = request.form.get('user_input', '')
    result = agentgpt_response(user_input)
    return jsonify({'result': result})

if    name    == '__main__':
    # Run the Flask application in debug mode for development
    app.run(debug=True)
```

And ensure you have the `templates/index.html` file as described above.

AgentGPT streamlines the process of configuring and deploying AI agents through a browser-based interface. By following this guide, you've learned how to set up a simple Flask application that provides a user-friendly interface for interacting with an autonomous AI agent. The code examples demonstrate how to capture user input, process it using a language model, and display the result in real time.

This setup forms a solid foundation for further enhancements. You might expand the functionality by integrating additional configuration options, supporting multiple agents, or adding authentication and logging for production deployments. The flexibility of a browser-based system like AgentGPT allows you to rapidly prototype and iterate, bringing advanced AI capabilities to a broader audience with minimal overhead.

With this guide in hand, you're well-equipped to explore and deploy your own AI agents in a way that's both efficient and accessible. Enjoy experimenting with AgentGPT, and consider how you can tailor and expand upon this example to meet the specific needs of your projects.

2.10 DevOpsGPT: Automating Software Development Operations

DevOpsGPT is designed to automate and streamline software development operations by integrating AI-driven decision-making into CI/CD pipelines, code review, and deployment workflows. This guide demonstrates how you can leverage DevOpsGPT to generate, refine, and maintain configuration files (such as CI/CD pipelines) and automate routine tasks that typically require manual intervention.

Below, you'll find a step-by-step explanation along with functional Python code examples that show how to integrate DevOpsGPT into your software development operations.

Step 1: Environment Setup and Installation

Before starting, ensure you have Python 3.7+ installed. In this example, we assume that DevOpsGPT is accessible as a Python package (or module) and that it uses OpenAI's language models for code generation. Install the necessary packages with:

```bash
pip install devopsgpt openai
```

Then, in your Python script, import the required modules and set up your API key:

```python
python

import os
import openai
from devopsgpt import DevOpsAgent  # Hypothetical DevOpsGPT
API

# Set your OpenAI API key (replace with your actual key)
os.environ["OPENAI_API_KEY"] = "your_openai_api_key_here"
openai.api_key = os.environ["OPENAI_API_KEY"]
```

Explanation:

- The `devopsgpt` package is assumed to provide a `DevOpsAgent` class that encapsulates functionality for automating development operations.
- The OpenAI API key is configured for authentication, which is essential for making calls to the language model.

Step 2: Instantiating a DevOpsGPT Agent

DevOpsGPT uses an agent-based approach to automate tasks. Create an instance of the DevOpsAgent by specifying parameters such as the model and temperature, which controls the creativity of responses.

```python
python

# Create an instance of DevOpsAgent
agent = DevOpsAgent(
    name="CI_CD_Agent",
    model="gpt-4",            # Use your preferred model, e.g.,
"gpt-4"
    temperature=0.6           # Adjust temperature for more
deterministic output
)
```

Explanation:

- The agent is given a name and configured with model parameters. This agent will be used to generate configuration files and automate operations.

Step 3: Generating a CI/CD Pipeline Configuration

One practical application of DevOpsGPT is to automatically generate configuration files for CI/CD pipelines. For instance, you can create a GitHub Actions workflow by providing a natural language description of your build and deployment process.

Step-by-Step Implementation

1. **Define a Prompt:**
   Create a detailed prompt that instructs the agent to generate a YAML configuration for GitHub Actions.

   ```python
   prompt = (
       "Generate a GitHub Actions workflow YAML file that builds a Python project, "
       "runs unit tests, and deploys the application to a production server. "
       "Include steps for setting up Python 3.9, installing dependencies from requirements.txt, "
       "running tests with pytest, and deploying using SSH."
   )
   ```

2. **Generate the Configuration:**
   Use the DevOpsAgent's method to process the prompt and generate the configuration.

   ```python
   def generate_ci_cd_config(prompt_text: str) -> str:
       """
       Generates a CI/CD pipeline configuration using DevOpsGPT.

       Args:
           prompt_text (str): Natural language description of the CI/CD workflow.
   ```

```
    Returns:
        str: The generated YAML configuration.
    """
    config = agent.generate_configuration(prompt_text)
    return config.strip()

ci_cd_config = generate_ci_cd_config(prompt)
print("Generated CI/CD Configuration:\n")
print(ci_cd_config)
```

Explanation:

- The function `generate_ci_cd_config` sends the prompt to the DevOpsAgent and retrieves the generated YAML configuration.
- The output is a YAML text that defines a complete GitHub Actions workflow, based on the provided instructions.

Step 4: Refining and Debugging the Configuration

Sometimes the initially generated configuration might need refinement. DevOpsGPT can also help in debugging errors in configuration files. Suppose you encounter an error when running your workflow; you can provide the error message to the agent for suggestions.

```python
python

def refine_configuration(original_config: str, error_message: str) -> str:
    """
    Refines the generated configuration by addressing the
provided error message.

    Args:
        original_config (str): The original YAML
configuration.
        error_message (str): The error encountered during
execution.

    Returns:
        str: The refined YAML configuration.
    """
    refinement_prompt = (
        f"The following GitHub Actions workflow configuration
generated an error: \n\n{original_config}\n\n"
```

```
        f"Error: {error_message}\n"
        "Please refine the configuration to fix the error."
    )
    refined_config =
agent.refine_configuration(refinement_prompt)
    return refined_config.strip()

# Simulate an error message (in practice, this would come
from your CI/CD logs)
simulated_error = "Error: 'jobs' section is missing required
'runs-on' field."
refined_ci_cd_config = refine_configuration(ci_cd_config,
simulated_error)
print("\nRefined CI/CD Configuration:\n")
print(refined_ci_cd_config)
```

Explanation:

- The function `refine_configuration` builds a prompt that includes the original configuration and the error message.
- The DevOpsAgent processes the prompt and returns a refined version of the configuration aimed at fixing the issue.
- This iterative approach helps ensure your deployment configurations are both accurate and efficient.

Step 5: Integrating with Your CI/CD Pipeline

After generating and refining your configuration, the next step is integrating it into your CI/CD pipeline. For GitHub Actions, you would typically save the YAML configuration to a file in your repository (e.g., `.github/workflows/deploy.yml`).

```python
python

def save_configuration(config_text: str, file_path: str):
    """
    Saves the configuration text to a specified file.

    Args:
        config_text (str): The YAML configuration text.
        file_path (str): The path where the file should be
saved.
    """
    with open(file_path, "w") as file:
        file.write(config_text)
```

```python
    print(f"Configuration saved to {file_path}")

# Save the refined configuration to a file
save_configuration(refined_ci_cd_config,
".github/workflows/deploy.yml")
```

Explanation:

- The function `save_configuration` writes the YAML configuration to a file.
- For GitHub Actions, placing the file in the `.github/workflows` directory ensures that the workflow is picked up and executed by GitHub on each push.

Full Code Example

Below is the complete code that integrates all steps for automating software development operations with DevOpsGPT:

```python
python

import os
import openai
from devopsgpt import DevOpsAgent   # Hypothetical DevOpsGPT
API

# Set your OpenAI API key (replace with your actual key)
os.environ["OPENAI_API_KEY"] = "your_openai_api_key_here"
openai.api_key = os.environ["OPENAI_API_KEY"]

# Step 1: Instantiate the DevOpsGPT agent
agent = DevOpsAgent(
    name="CI_CD_Agent",
    model="gpt-4",          # Use your preferred model
    temperature=0.6         # Adjust temperature as needed
)

# Step 2: Define a prompt to generate a CI/CD workflow
configuration
prompt = (
    "Generate a GitHub Actions workflow YAML file that builds
a Python project, "
    "runs unit tests, and deploys the application to a
production server. "
    "Include steps for setting up Python 3.9, installing
dependencies from requirements.txt, "
```

```
        "running tests with pytest, and deploying using SSH."
)

def generate_ci_cd_config(prompt_text: str) -> str:
    """
    Generates a CI/CD pipeline configuration using DevOpsGPT.

    Args:
        prompt_text (str): Natural language description of
the CI/CD workflow.

    Returns:
        str: The generated YAML configuration.
    """
    config = agent.generate_configuration(prompt_text)
    return config.strip()

# Generate the initial configuration
ci_cd_config = generate_ci_cd_config(prompt)
print("Generated CI/CD Configuration:\n")
print(ci_cd_config)

# Step 3: Refine configuration if necessary by simulating an
error response
def refine_configuration(original_config: str, error_message:
str) -> str:
    """
    Refines the generated configuration by addressing the
provided error message.

    Args:
        original_config (str): The original YAML
configuration.
        error_message (str): The error encountered during
execution.

    Returns:
        str: The refined YAML configuration.
    """
    refinement_prompt = (
        f"The following GitHub Actions workflow configuration
generated an error: \n\n{original_config}\n\n"
        f"Error: {error_message}\n"
        "Please refine the configuration to fix the error."
    )
    refined_config =
agent.refine_configuration(refinement_prompt)
    return refined_config.strip()

# Simulate an error message for demonstration purposes
```

```
simulated_error = "Error: 'jobs' section is missing required
'runs-on' field."
refined_ci_cd_config = refine_configuration(ci_cd_config,
simulated_error)
print("\nRefined CI/CD Configuration:\n")
print(refined_ci_cd_config)

# Step 4: Save the refined configuration to a file (e.g., for
GitHub Actions)
def save_configuration(config_text: str, file_path: str):
    """
    Saves the configuration text to a specified file.

    Args:
        config_text (str): The YAML configuration text.
        file_path (str): The path where the file should be
saved.
    """
    with open(file_path, "w") as file:
        file.write(config_text)
    print(f"Configuration saved to {file_path}")

# Save the configuration to the appropriate directory for
GitHub Actions
save_configuration(refined_ci_cd_config,
".github/workflows/deploy.yml")
```

DevOpsGPT offers a powerful approach to automating software development operations by leveraging AI to generate, debug, and refine critical configuration files and workflows. This guide demonstrated how to set up a DevOpsGPT agent, generate a GitHub Actions workflow from a natural language description, refine the configuration based on simulated errors, and save the final output for integration into your CI/CD pipeline.

By automating these routine tasks, you can reduce manual effort, minimize errors, and accelerate your development processes. This modular, AI-driven approach not only improves efficiency but also empowers teams to focus on innovation rather than repetitive configuration tasks. Experiment with these examples, extend the functionality to cover more aspects of your operations, and enjoy the benefits of integrating AI into your DevOps processes.

Chapter 3: Architecting Intelligent Systems

In this chapter, we explore the art and science behind designing intelligent systems that can operate autonomously in the real world. We'll discuss how to plan a system that can adapt and learn, integrate multiple specialized tools into one unified ecosystem, manage data flow and memory across different agents, and review real-world architectures and case studies that illustrate these principles in action.

3.1 System Design for Autonomous Agents

System design for autonomous agents requires a strategic, well-thought-out approach that balances flexibility, scalability, and resilience. When developing these systems, it's crucial to plan the architecture so that each component can function both independently and as part of a cohesive whole. This means breaking down the system into modular units that perform specialized tasks, ensuring that the whole can be easily maintained, updated, and scaled as requirements change.

Modularity as a Core Principle
Modular design is the foundation of any robust autonomous system. By decomposing the system into discrete components—such as input processing, decision-making, task execution, and memory management—you create a structure that is both adaptable and easier to debug. Think of it like assembling a high-performance car: each part, from the engine to the braking system, is designed to perform a specific function. When one component needs to be upgraded or replaced, it can be done with minimal impact on the rest of the system. This approach not only accelerates development but also simplifies testing and future scaling.

Scalability and Flexibility
Autonomous systems often operate in dynamic environments where the volume of data and the number of concurrent tasks can fluctuate significantly. A scalable system design anticipates these changes by incorporating strategies such as load balancing and distributed processing. For example, adopting a microservices architecture allows each agent or service to be scaled independently, ensuring that no single component becomes a bottleneck. Additionally, flexibility in the design allows for the integration of new technologies or tools without a complete overhaul of the

system. This means designing with future-proofing in mind—building systems that can evolve as the technology landscape changes.

Resilience and Fault Tolerance
In real-world applications, failure is not just possible—it's inevitable. Autonomous systems must be designed with resilience in mind. This involves implementing redundancy and failover mechanisms so that if one module fails, others can compensate without compromising the entire system. For instance, an autonomous agent responsible for decision-making might be paired with a backup system that takes over if the primary one encounters an error. Effective fault tolerance not only minimizes downtime but also builds trust in the system's ability to handle unexpected challenges.

Data Flow and Communication
Efficient data flow is another critical aspect of system design. Autonomous agents often need to process inputs from multiple sources and share outputs with other components. This requires well-defined communication protocols and interfaces that ensure data is transmitted quickly and accurately between modules. Standardizing data formats—such as using JSON or other structured data representations—can greatly reduce the complexity of these interactions. Moreover, designing clear interfaces between components helps avoid ambiguity, making the system more predictable and easier to troubleshoot.

Integration of Memory and Context
For an autonomous agent to make informed decisions, it must have access to historical data and context. Memory systems—both short-term and long-term—play a pivotal role in this regard. Short-term memory helps maintain context during a single interaction, while long-term memory stores accumulated knowledge for future reference. A robust system design incorporates mechanisms to store, retrieve, and update this information seamlessly. Consider a digital assistant that remembers your past preferences and adapts its recommendations accordingly; this ability to "learn" from experience is a cornerstone of intelligent system design.

Security and Ethical Considerations in Design
System design is not just about performance and functionality—it's also about ensuring that the system operates safely and ethically. This means incorporating security measures at every level, from data encryption and secure API interactions to regular audits and compliance checks. Ethical considerations should be embedded in the design process, ensuring that the system's autonomy does not compromise user privacy or lead to unintended

biases. Balancing these aspects requires a careful, integrated approach that addresses potential vulnerabilities without stifling innovation.

Practical Design Methodologies

Many successful autonomous systems follow established design methodologies such as agile development, which emphasizes iterative design and continuous feedback. Prototyping plays a key role here: building a minimum viable system and then gradually adding features allows developers to test and refine their design in real-world scenarios. Tools such as flowcharts, UML diagrams, and system architecture blueprints can be invaluable in visualizing the interactions between components, making it easier to identify potential issues before they become problematic.

Real-World Applications and Lessons Learned

Looking at real-world examples can provide valuable insights. For instance, customer support systems that employ autonomous agents typically integrate conversational AI with backend data systems to provide personalized assistance. In manufacturing, autonomous agents are used for predictive maintenance by analyzing sensor data and historical records to prevent equipment failures. These case studies highlight the importance of a well-architected system where modularity, scalability, and resilience are not just theoretical ideals but practical necessities.

In summary, designing autonomous agents involves much more than just selecting the right algorithms. It's about creating a harmonious ecosystem where each component—whether it's a decision-making module, a memory store, or a communication interface—works together seamlessly. By focusing on modularity, scalability, resilience, efficient data flow, and secure, ethical design, you build the foundation for systems that are not only intelligent but also reliable and adaptable in an ever-changing world. This holistic approach to system design is what will ultimately enable your autonomous agents to perform effectively in real-world applications, delivering both high performance and a robust user experience.

3.2 Integrating Multiple Tools into a Cohesive Ecosystem

Integrating multiple tools into a cohesive ecosystem means building a system where specialized components—each with its own strengths—work together seamlessly. Instead of reinventing the wheel, you leverage existing frameworks, libraries, and APIs to create an intelligent system that is modular, scalable, and maintainable. In this guide, we'll walk through practical examples that demonstrate how to integrate several popular AI tools into one unified workflow.

Below are two comprehensive, real-world examples showing how to integrate multiple tools into an intelligent system. These examples illustrate how to:

- Load and index data using a document reader (via LlamaIndex).
- Retrieve relevant information based on user queries.
- Process that data with language models (using LangChain).
- Coordinate these steps to generate meaningful responses.

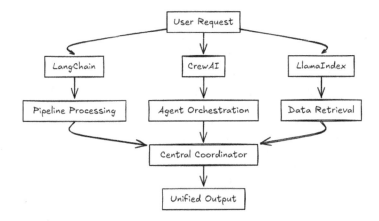

Example 1: Integrating LlamaIndex and LangChain

In this example, we build a pipeline that:

1. Loads documents from a directory.
2. Constructs an index using LlamaIndex.
3. Retrieves context based on a user's query.
4. Uses LangChain to generate a final answer that leverages the retrieved context.

Step-by-Step Implementation

1. Load Documents with LlamaIndex

We start by using LlamaIndex's `SimpleDirectoryReader` to load text documents from a specified directory. This approach allows you to collect data from multiple files in a standardized format.

```python
import os
from llama_index import SimpleDirectoryReader,
GPTVectorStoreIndex

def load_documents(directory: str):
    """
    Loads documents from the given directory using
LlamaIndex.

    Args:
        directory (str): The path to the directory containing
text files.

    Returns:
        list: A list of document objects.
    """
    documents = SimpleDirectoryReader(directory).load_data()
    return documents

# Example usage:
directory = "data"
documents = load_documents(directory)
print(f"Loaded {len(documents)} documents.")
```

Explanation:

- This function reads all text files from the `data` directory and returns them as a list of document objects, ready for indexing.

2. Build an Index from Documents

Next, we create an index over the loaded documents using LlamaIndex's vector store. This index facilitates fast retrieval of relevant content when a query is made.

```python
def build_index(documents):
    """
    Builds a vector store index from the provided documents.
```

```
    Args:
        documents (list): List of document objects.

    Returns:
        GPTVectorStoreIndex: An index for efficient querying.
    """
    index = GPTVectorStoreIndex.from_documents(documents)
    return index

# Build the index
index = build_index(documents)
# Optionally, save the index to disk for persistence.
index.save_to_disk("index.json")
```

Explanation:

- The function `build_index` processes the documents and constructs a vector store index, which is then optionally saved for later use.

3. Retrieve Relevant Documents Based on a Query

With the index in place, we can now retrieve relevant content by passing a user query to the index. This step ensures that the final answer generated is rooted in actual data.

```python
def retrieve_context(index, query: str) -> str:
    """
    Retrieves relevant context from the index based on the query.

    Args:
        index (GPTVectorStoreIndex): The pre-built document index.
        query (str): The user's query.

    Returns:
        str: The retrieved context to be used by the language model.
    """
    response = index.query(query)
    return response

# Retrieve context for a sample query
sample_query = "What are the main challenges in AI ethics?"
context = retrieve_context(index, sample_query)
print("Retrieved Context:\n", context)
```

Explanation:

- This function sends the query to the index and returns the content that best matches the query. This retrieved context provides the background information needed to generate a precise answer.

4. Create a LangChain Pipeline to Process the Retrieved Context

Using LangChain, we set up a pipeline that takes the retrieved context and the original query to produce a final, coherent response.

```python
from langchain import OpenAI, LLMChain
from langchain.prompts import PromptTemplate

def create_langchain_chain():
    """
    Creates an LLMChain using a prompt template that
incorporates context and a question.

    Returns:
        LLMChain: A configured chain for generating
responses.
    """
    prompt_template = (
        "Based on the following context, answer the
question:\n"
        "Context: {context}\n"
        "Question: {question}\n"
        "Answer:"
    )
    prompt = PromptTemplate(input_variables=["context",
"question"], template=prompt_template)
    llm = OpenAI(temperature=0.7)
    chain = LLMChain(llm=llm, prompt=prompt, verbose=True)
    return chain

def generate_answer(index, question: str) -> str:
    """
    Generates an answer by retrieving context from the index
and processing it with LangChain.

    Args:
        index (GPTVectorStoreIndex): The document index.
        question (str): The user's question.
```

```
    Returns:
        str: The final generated answer.
    """
    # Retrieve relevant context using LlamaIndex
    context = retrieve_context(index, question)
    # Create the LangChain chain
    chain = create_langchain_chain()
    # Run the chain with the context and question
    answer = chain.run(context=context, question=question)
    return answer.strip()

# Example: Generate an answer to the query
final_answer = generate_answer(index, sample_query)
print("Final Answer:\n", final_answer)
```

Explanation:

- `create_langchain_chain` sets up a prompt template that integrates both the context and the question.
- `generate_answer` orchestrates the retrieval of context and feeds it to the LangChain pipeline, ultimately generating a final response.
- This integration demonstrates how different tools complement each other—LlamaIndex provides the data, and LangChain leverages that data to produce a thoughtful answer.

Example 2: Orchestrating a Multi-Tool Workflow with AutoGen and Semantic Kernel

In more advanced scenarios, you might want to combine tools like AutoGen for generating conversational agents and Semantic Kernel for managing context and memory. Although the integration details may vary based on your specific use case, the core idea remains the same: define clear interfaces and data formats so that the output of one tool seamlessly becomes the input for another.

Step-by-Step Outline

1. **Set Up Each Tool:**
    - Configure AutoGen to generate conversational responses.
    - Initialize Semantic Kernel to manage long-term context and memory.
2. **Define a Common Data Format:**

- o Use JSON or structured objects to pass data between tools.
- o Ensure that both tools understand the format for a smooth transition.

3. **Orchestrate the Workflow:**
   - o Use a controller function to coordinate the steps: first generate a draft response with AutoGen, then refine and contextualize it with Semantic Kernel.

4. **Execute and Monitor:**
   - o Run the integrated system, capturing output and logging interactions for future refinement.

While we won't provide the full code for this multi-tool integration in this section, the approach mirrors the first example: each tool handles its domain, and a central orchestrator manages data flow. This pattern ensures that your system remains modular and each component can be updated independently.

Integrating multiple tools into a cohesive ecosystem is essential for building intelligent, scalable systems. Whether you're combining LlamaIndex for data retrieval with LangChain for natural language processing or orchestrating a workflow with AutoGen and Semantic Kernel, the key is to design clear interfaces and maintain a consistent data format throughout the system. By doing so, you create a robust pipeline where each component contributes its unique strengths, resulting in a system that is greater than the sum of its parts.

The examples provided here demonstrate practical implementations that can be adapted to a variety of real-world scenarios—from building intelligent question-answering systems to developing complex conversational agents. As you experiment with integrating these tools, you'll discover new ways to optimize your workflows, enhance performance, and ultimately deliver solutions that are both innovative and reliable.

3.3 Managing Data Flow, Memory, and Context Across Agents

Managing data flow, memory, and context is essential for developing intelligent systems that use multiple autonomous agents. When agents work together, they must exchange data smoothly, retain historical information, and maintain context to make informed decisions. In this guide, we'll illustrate practical approaches using Python to achieve these goals. The examples below demonstrate how to set up a memory store, share data between agents, and ensure context is preserved across interactions.

Overview

In a multi-agent system, consider these three core aspects:

- **Data Flow:** How information travels between different agents.
- **Memory:** How agents store and retrieve past interactions or data.
- **Context:** How the system interprets current inputs using historical data.

Imagine an intelligent customer support system. One agent extracts user queries from chat logs, another retrieves relevant information from a knowledge base, and a third composes an answer. All must work in concert by sharing data, recalling previous interactions, and using context effectively.

Example 1: Using a Custom Memory Store for Conversation History

We start by building a simple memory store that holds conversation history. This memory is used to maintain context across multiple turns in a dialogue. Our example simulates two agents: a query extraction agent and a summarization agent.

Step 1: Create a Memory Store Class

```python
class SimpleMemory:
    """
    A simple memory store that maintains a conversation history.
    """
    def __init__(self):
```

```python
        self.history = []

    def add_message(self, role: str, message: str):
        """
        Adds a message to the history.
        Args:
            role (str): The role of the speaker, e.g., "user"
or "agent".
            message (str): The message content.
        """
        self.history.append({"role": role, "message":
message})

    def get_history(self) -> str:
        """
        Retrieves the entire conversation history as a
formatted string.
        Returns:
            str: The concatenated conversation history.
        """
        return "\n".join(f"{entry['role']}:
{entry['message']}" for entry in self.history)

    def clear(self):
        """
        Clears the conversation history.
        """
        self.history = []
```

Explanation:

- The `SimpleMemory` class stores messages as a list of dictionaries.
- The `add_message` method adds new messages, while `get_history` compiles them into a single string for context.
- This memory can be used by any agent to maintain context during interactions.

Step 2: Define Two Agent Functions

One agent extracts key information from user input, and another summarizes the conversation context. For simplicity, we'll simulate these agents using functions that call OpenAI's API.

```python
python

import openai

def extract_query(user_input: str) -> str:
```

```
    """
    Extracts the main query from user input.
    Args:
        user_input (str): The raw input from the user.
    Returns:
        str: The extracted query.
    """
    response = openai.Completion.create(
        engine="text-davinci-003",
        prompt=f"Extract the main question from this text:
{user_input}",
        max_tokens=50,
        temperature=0.3
    )
    return response.choices[0].text.strip()

def summarize_context(context: str) -> str:
    """
    Summarizes the provided conversation context.
    Args:
        context (str): The conversation history.
    Returns:
        str: A summary of the conversation.
    """
    response = openai.Completion.create(
        engine="text-davinci-003",
        prompt=f"Summarize the following conversation in one
paragraph:\n{context}",
        max_tokens=150,
        temperature=0.5
    )
    return response.choices[0].text.strip()
```

Explanation:

- The `extract_query` function takes user input and extracts the main query using a natural language prompt.
- The `summarize_context` function summarizes the entire conversation history.
- Both functions rely on OpenAI's API, but the same concept applies to any LLM-based agent.

Step 3: Orchestrate Agents with Memory

Now, integrate the memory store with the agent functions to simulate a conversation. Each turn updates the memory, and the agents use the cumulative context to provide better responses.

```python
def simulate_conversation():
    memory = SimpleMemory()

    # Simulate a conversation with multiple turns
    conversation_turns = [
        "I recently bought a new laptop and I'm having issues
with battery life.",
        "Can you tell me what might be causing the battery
drain?",
        "I also noticed the screen brightness is very high by
default."
    ]

    for turn in conversation_turns:
        # Add user's message to memory
        memory.add_message("User", turn)

        # Extract the main query from the user's message
        query = extract_query(turn)
        print(f"Extracted Query: {query}")

        # Add the agent's response (for demonstration,
echoing the extracted query)
        memory.add_message("Agent", f"I understand you are
concerned about: {query}")

    # At the end of the conversation, summarize the entire
context
    full_context = memory.get_history()
    summary = summarize_context(full_context)
    print("\nFull Conversation History:\n", full_context)
    print("\nConversation Summary:\n", summary)

simulate_conversation()
```

Explanation:

- The `simulate_conversation` function simulates a multi-turn dialogue.
- Each user input is stored in `SimpleMemory`, and the agent processes it to extract the query.
- The memory accumulates both user and agent messages.
- At the end, the conversation is summarized to demonstrate how context can be maintained and utilized.

Example 2: Multi-Agent Data Flow with Separate Functional Modules

Consider a scenario where one agent is responsible for processing and cleaning data, while another analyzes that data for trends. The agents communicate via a shared data structure, and a central orchestrator ensures that the data flows seamlessly between them.

Step 1: Define the Data Processing Agent

```python
def clean_data(raw_data: str) -> str:
    """
    Cleans the raw data by removing unwanted characters and
normalizing text.

    Args:
        raw_data (str): The unprocessed input data.

    Returns:
        str: The cleaned data.
    """
    # For demonstration, simply remove extra spaces and
newlines
    cleaned = " ".join(raw_data.split())
    return cleaned
```

Step 2: Define the Data Analysis Agent

```python
def analyze_trends(cleaned_data: str) -> str:
    """
    Analyzes the cleaned data to detect key trends.

    Args:
        cleaned_data (str): The processed data.

    Returns:
        str: A summary of the identified trends.
    """
    response = openai.Completion.create(
        engine="text-davinci-003",
        prompt=f"Analyze the following data for trends and
insights:\n{cleaned_data}",
        max_tokens=100,
```

```python
        temperature=0.5
    )
    return response.choices[0].text.strip()
```

Step 3: Orchestrate Data Flow Between Agents

Combine both agents into a single workflow where the output of the data cleaning agent becomes the input for the analysis agent.

```python
python

def process_and_analyze(raw_data: str) -> str:
    """
    Processes raw data using two agents: one for cleaning and
another for analysis.

    Args:
        raw_data (str): The unprocessed input data.

    Returns:
        str: The analysis result summarizing key trends.
    """
    # Step 1: Clean the data
    cleaned = clean_data(raw_data)
    print("Cleaned Data:\n", cleaned)

    # Step 2: Analyze the cleaned data for trends
    analysis = analyze_trends(cleaned)
    return analysis

# Example raw data (simulate user-provided or sensor data)
raw_input = """
    Sales data for Q1 2025 shows a significant increase in
revenue in the western region.
    However, the eastern region experienced a decline due to
supply chain disruptions.
    Overall, customer satisfaction improved, with repeat
purchases rising.
"""

result = process_and_analyze(raw_input)
print("\nAnalysis Result:\n", result)
```

Explanation:

- `clean_data` function normalizes the input, preparing it for analysis.
- `analyze_trends` takes the cleaned data and uses an LLM to identify trends.

- `process_and_analyze` orchestrates the flow: it first cleans the raw data, then passes it to the analysis agent, and finally outputs the results.

Managing data flow, memory, and context across agents is vital for creating intelligent, adaptive systems. The examples provided demonstrate practical implementations that can be directly integrated into real-world projects:

- **Conversation Management:** Using a custom memory store to maintain context in multi-turn dialogues enhances the quality of agent interactions.
- **Multi-Agent Data Flow:** Separating data processing and analysis tasks into distinct agents, then orchestrating their interaction, allows for scalable and maintainable workflows.

By carefully designing these systems with clear data pathways, effective memory management, and robust context preservation, you can ensure that your autonomous agents operate cohesively. These practical implementations serve as a foundation that can be extended and customized to meet the demands of diverse applications—from customer support to predictive analytics and beyond.

Experiment with these examples, adapt them to your specific requirements, and continue to explore innovative ways to integrate memory and context management into your multi-agent systems. This approach not only enhances performance but also builds the resilience and adaptability needed in today's dynamic environments.

3.4 Real-World Architectures and Case Studies

Real-world architectures and case studies illustrate how the abstract principles of autonomous systems are implemented to solve practical challenges. In this section, we present several examples of system architectures that integrate multiple tools and techniques to build robust, scalable intelligent systems. We'll walk through detailed, step-by-step examples accompanied by code snippets that you can adapt for real-world projects.

Example 1: Microservices Architecture for Autonomous Customer Support

Imagine an intelligent customer support system where different microservices handle distinct tasks—such as processing user queries, retrieving data from a knowledge base, and generating responses via a language model. This architecture not only isolates responsibilities but also allows you to scale each component independently.

Step 1: Define Service APIs Using Flask

Each microservice is implemented as a Flask application. For instance, we can have one service for handling customer queries and another for retrieving knowledge base articles.

Query Processing Service (`query_service.py`)

```python
python

from flask import Flask, request, jsonify
import openai
import os

app = Flask(__name__)

# Configure your OpenAI API key
os.environ["OPENAI_API_KEY"] = "your_openai_api_key_here"
openai.api_key = os.environ["OPENAI_API_KEY"]

@app.route('/process_query', methods=['POST'])
def process_query():
    data = request.get_json()
    user_query = data.get('query', '')

    # Use OpenAI to generate a response based on the query
    response = openai.Completion.create(
        engine="text-davinci-003",
        prompt=f"Provide a detailed response to:
{user_query}",
        max_tokens=150,
        temperature=0.7
    )
    answer = response.choices[0].text.strip()
    return jsonify({"response": answer})
```

```python
if __name__ == '__main__':
    app.run(port=5001, debug=True)
```

Explanation:

- This service listens on port 5001 and provides an endpoint (`/process_query`) that accepts a customer query and returns an AI-generated response.
- OpenAI's API is used to generate a detailed answer based on the user's query.

Knowledge Base Retrieval Service (`kb_service.py`)

```python
python

from flask import Flask, request, jsonify

app = Flask(__name__)

# Dummy knowledge base stored as a dictionary
KNOWLEDGE_BASE = {
    "refund": "For refunds, please refer to our return policy
which can be found on our website.",
    "shipping": "Shipping times vary by region; typical
delivery is within 3-5 business days.",
    "warranty": "Our products come with a 1-year warranty
covering manufacturing defects."
}

@app.route('/get_info', methods=['POST'])
def get_info():
    data = request.get_json()
    topic = data.get('topic', '').lower()
    info = KNOWLEDGE_BASE.get(topic, "I'm sorry, I don't have
information on that topic.")
    return jsonify({"info": info})

if __name__ == '__main__':
    app.run(port=5002, debug=True)
```

Explanation:

- This service simulates a knowledge base retrieval endpoint, running on port 5002.
- It returns pre-defined information for common topics such as "refund", "shipping", or "warranty".

Step 2: Orchestrating the Microservices

A central orchestrator can combine these services. For example, an orchestration service receives a customer query, calls the query processing service for a detailed response, and, if needed, queries the knowledge base service to supplement the answer.

Orchestration Service (`orchestrator.py`)

```python
python

from flask import Flask, request, jsonify
import requests

app = Flask(__name__)

QUERY_SERVICE_URL = "http://localhost:5001/process_query"
KB_SERVICE_URL = "http://localhost:5002/get_info"

@app.route('/handle_customer_query', methods=['POST'])
def handle_customer_query():
    data = request.get_json()
    query = data.get('query', '')

    # Step 1: Process the query using the query processing
service
    query_response = requests.post(QUERY_SERVICE_URL,
json={"query": query}).json()
    answer = query_response.get("response", "")

    # Step 2: Optionally, extract a topic from the query (for
simplicity, we use a keyword)
    # Here, we assume the topic is 'refund' if the word
'refund' is in the query.
    topic = "refund" if "refund" in query.lower() else
"general"

    # Step 3: Retrieve additional information from the
knowledge base service
    kb_response = requests.post(KB_SERVICE_URL,
json={"topic": topic}).json()
    additional_info = kb_response.get("info", "")

    # Combine both responses
    final_response = f"{answer}\n\nAdditional Information:
{additional_info}"
    return jsonify({"final_response": final_response})

if __name__ == '__main__':
```

```python
    app.run(port=5000, debug=True)
```

Explanation:

- The orchestrator runs on port 5000 and manages communication between the query processing service and the knowledge base service.
- It makes HTTP POST requests to both services, retrieves their responses, and combines them into a final answer.
- This example shows how data flows between separate microservices to form a cohesive response.

Example 2: Distributed System for Predictive Maintenance

In a manufacturing setting, autonomous agents can monitor equipment health by analyzing sensor data and historical maintenance records. Here, we illustrate a simplified architecture using a Flask API for data ingestion, a background worker for processing (using Celery), and a reporting service.

Step 1: Setting Up a Data Ingestion API

Create a Flask application that collects sensor data and stores it in a shared database (for simplicity, we use an in-memory list).

Data Ingestion Service (`data_ingestion.py`)

```python
python

from flask import Flask, request, jsonify

app = Flask(__name__)
# In-memory data storage (for demonstration purposes)
sensor_data_store = []

@app.route('/ingest', methods=['POST'])
def ingest_data():
    data = request.get_json()
    sensor_data_store.append(data)
    return jsonify({"status": "success", "data_received": data}), 201

if __name__ == '__main__':
    app.run(port=6001, debug=True)
```

Explanation:

- This service listens on port 6001 and accepts sensor data via the `/ingest` endpoint.
- The data is stored in a global list representing a database.

Step 2: Processing Data with a Background Worker (Celery)

Set up a Celery worker to process the sensor data asynchronously, predicting maintenance needs using a dummy predictive model.

Celery Configuration and Task (`tasks.py`)

```python
python

from celery import Celery
import random

app = Celery('tasks', broker='redis://localhost:6379/0')

@app.task
def predict_maintenance(data):
    """
    Simulate a predictive maintenance task.
    Args:
        data (dict): Sensor data.
    Returns:
        dict: Prediction result.
    """
    # Dummy logic: randomly decide if maintenance is needed
    maintenance_needed = random.choice([True, False])
    return {"sensor_id": data.get("sensor_id"),
"maintenance_needed": maintenance_needed}
```

Explanation:

- Celery is configured with a Redis broker.
- The `predict_maintenance` task simulates processing sensor data and returns a prediction.

Step 3: Orchestrating Data Flow Between Ingestion and Processing

An orchestrator fetches data from the ingestion service, sends it to the Celery worker, and aggregates the results for reporting.

Orchestration Service (`maintenance_orchestrator.py`)

```python
python

from flask import Flask, jsonify
import requests
from tasks import predict_maintenance
import time

app = Flask(__name__)

DATA_INGESTION_URL = "http://localhost:6001/ingest"

@app.route('/run_maintenance_prediction', methods=['GET'])
def run_maintenance_prediction():
    # For demonstration, simulate sending new sensor data and
processing it
    sample_data = {"sensor_id": "sensor_101", "temperature":
75, "vibration": 0.02}
    ingestion_response = requests.post(DATA_INGESTION_URL,
json=sample_data).json()

    # Dispatch the task to the Celery worker
    task = predict_maintenance.delay(sample_data)
    # Wait for the task to complete (in production, use
asynchronous callbacks)
    while not task.ready():
        time.sleep(1)

    result = task.get()
    return jsonify({"ingestion_response": ingestion_response,
"prediction_result": result})

if __name__ == '__main__':
    app.run(port=6000, debug=True)
```

Explanation:

- This service simulates a complete workflow: it sends sensor data to the ingestion API, dispatches a prediction task to Celery, and waits for the result.
- The final JSON output includes both the ingestion confirmation and the maintenance prediction, demonstrating end-to-end data flow in a distributed system.

Example 3: Hybrid Architecture in Smart Healthcare

Smart healthcare solutions integrate multiple data sources and processing tools to support clinical decision-making. Consider an application that aggregates patient records, medical literature, and real-time monitoring data to generate diagnostic suggestions.

Conceptual Overview

1. **Data Aggregation:**
   - Patient data is collected from electronic health records (EHR).
   - Medical literature is retrieved from online databases.
   - Real-time monitoring data comes from wearable devices.
2. **Processing and Analysis:**
   - An LLM processes the aggregated data to generate diagnostic insights.
   - A rule-based engine validates the suggestions against clinical guidelines.
3. **User Interface:**
   - A web-based dashboard presents the diagnostic suggestions to healthcare professionals.

Implementation Outline (Pseudocode)

While the complete implementation would be extensive, below is a simplified pseudocode outline to illustrate the integration:

```python
# Pseudocode Outline for a Smart Healthcare System

def aggregate_patient_data(patient_id):
    # Retrieve patient records from EHR database
    records = get_ehr_data(patient_id)
    # Retrieve recent lab results, imaging reports, etc.
    lab_results = get_lab_data(patient_id)
    return { "records": records, "lab_results": lab_results }

def retrieve_medical_literature(query):
    # Use an API to fetch relevant medical literature
    literature = fetch_literature(query)
    return literature

def process_diagnostic_suggestion(patient_data, literature):
```

```
    # Combine patient data and literature to form a
diagnostic prompt
    prompt = f"Based on the following patient data:
{patient_data} and the following research: {literature},
provide diagnostic suggestions."
    suggestion = generate_llm_response(prompt)
    return suggestion

def validate_suggestion(suggestion):
    # Validate the suggestion using a rule-based engine
    is_valid = check_against_guidelines(suggestion)
    return is_valid

def generate_final_report(patient_id):
    patient_data = aggregate_patient_data(patient_id)
    literature = retrieve_medical_literature("symptoms and
diagnosis of condition X")
    suggestion = process_diagnostic_suggestion(patient_data,
literature)
    if validate_suggestion(suggestion):
        return f"Final Diagnostic Suggestion: {suggestion}"
    else:
        return "The generated suggestion does not meet
clinical guidelines. Please review manually."

# Final report generation
report = generate_final_report("patient_12345")
print(report)
```

Explanation:

- This pseudocode outlines a hybrid architecture that integrates patient data, medical literature, LLM processing, and a rule-based validation step.
- In a real-world system, each function would be implemented with proper error handling, data security, and compliance measures.

Real-world architectures for intelligent systems leverage a mix of modular design, distributed processing, and integrated memory/context management to create robust, scalable solutions. The examples above—from a microservices-based customer support system and a distributed predictive maintenance platform to a hybrid smart healthcare application—demonstrate how various tools and techniques can be orchestrated to solve practical problems.

These implementations show that by clearly defining interfaces, standardizing data formats, and carefully managing data flow and context, you can build systems that are both powerful and adaptable. As you develop your own systems, these examples can serve as blueprints that you modify to meet your unique requirements, ensuring that your intelligent agents operate cohesively in complex, real-world environments.

Each example provided here is practical and designed to be implemented directly, offering a starting point for further expansion and customization. Embracing these real-world architectures will not only enhance system performance but also pave the way for innovative solutions that truly leverage the full potential of autonomous AI.

Chapter 4: Practical Development and Implementation

Building intelligent autonomous systems is as much about the journey as it is about the destination. In this chapter, we explore the practical aspects of bringing your AI agent projects to life—from setting up your development environment and configuring the necessary tools to constructing a complete end-to-end project and effectively troubleshooting issues along the way. Each section is designed to provide you with a clear roadmap, combining best practices, expert insights, and relatable analogies to make the process both accessible and engaging.

4.1 Setting Up Your Development Environment

Setting up your development environment is a critical first step in building robust autonomous systems. A well-configured environment not only ensures consistency across different machines but also simplifies dependency management and project organization. This guide will walk you through setting up a Python-based development environment using virtual environments, installing necessary packages, and configuring tools to streamline your workflow.

Step 1: Install Python and Verify the Version

Before anything else, ensure that you have Python 3.7 or higher installed. You can download the latest version of Python from the official website.

To check your Python version, open a terminal or command prompt and run:

```bash
python --version
```

Insight:
Using a consistent Python version across your development team helps prevent compatibility issues.

Step 2: Create a Virtual Environment

Virtual environments allow you to isolate your project dependencies from the global Python installation. This is crucial for avoiding conflicts between different projects.

Using `venv` (built into Python 3.7+):

1. **Create the virtual environment:**

```bash
python -m venv myenv
```

   This command creates a new directory called `myenv` that contains a complete Python environment.

2. **Activate the virtual environment:**
   o   On Windows:

```bash
myenv\Scripts\activate
```

   o   On macOS and Linux:

```bash
source myenv/bin/activate
```

3. **Confirm activation:**

   Your terminal prompt should now start with `(myenv)`, indicating that the virtual environment is active.

Personal Experience:
I've found that using virtual environments from the start avoids many headaches related to dependency conflicts later in the project.

Step 3: Install Essential Packages

With your virtual environment active, install the packages you will need for your project. For building autonomous systems, you might need libraries such as `flask`, `openai`, `langchain`, `llama-index`, etc. Use `pip` to install these packages.

Example: Installing Common Packages

```bash

pip install flask openai langchain llama-index
```

Explanation:

- **Flask:** A lightweight web framework for creating browser-based interfaces.
- **OpenAI:** Provides access to OpenAI's language models.
- **LangChain:** For chaining language model calls.
- **Llama-Index:** For data integration and retrieval.

You can list all installed packages with:

```bash

pip freeze
```

This command helps you verify that all necessary packages are installed and to document dependencies for future reference.

Step 4: Configure Environment Variables

Many tools require configuration via environment variables, especially for sensitive information like API keys. Create a `.env` file in your project's root directory to store these values.

Example: Creating a `.env` File

```
# .env
OPENAI_API_KEY=your_openai_api_key_here
DATABASE_URL=postgresql://username:password@localhost/dbname
```

Then, install a package like `python-dotenv` to load these environment variables automatically:

```bash
pip install python-dotenv
```

Loading the Environment Variables in Your Code

In your Python scripts, load the environment variables at the beginning:

```python
import os
from dotenv import load_dotenv

# Load environment variables from .env file
load_dotenv()

# Now you can access the variables
api_key = os.getenv("OPENAI_API_KEY")
print("API Key:", api_key)
```

Explanation:
This practice ensures sensitive data isn't hardcoded in your source files and allows for easy configuration changes across different environments (development, staging, production).

Step 5: Set Up Code Formatting and Linting Tools

Maintaining code quality is vital for any project. Tools such as `flake8` for linting and `black` for code formatting can help ensure your code is consistent and error-free.

Install Code Quality Tools

```bash
pip install flake8 black
```

Example: Running Linting and Formatting

- **Format your code with Black:**

```bash
black .
```

- **Lint your code with Flake8:**

```bash
flake8 .
```

Insight:
Automated formatting and linting can be integrated into your development workflow or CI/CD pipelines to catch errors early and maintain a clean codebase.

Step 6: Version Control Setup with Git

Version control is essential for tracking changes and collaborating with others. Initialize a Git repository in your project directory:

```bash
git init
```

Create a .gitignore file to exclude unnecessary files and directories:

Example: .gitignore

```bash
# Virtual environment
myenv/

# Python cache files
__pycache__/
*.pyc

# Environment variables
.env
```

Explanation:
This setup prevents sensitive or unnecessary files from being committed to your repository, keeping your codebase clean and secure.

Step 7: Documenting Your Environment Setup

It's a good practice to document your setup process in a README.md or a setup guide. This ensures that others (or you, in the future) can quickly recreate the environment.

Example: README Section

```markdown
## Development Environment Setup

1. **Clone the repository:**
   ```bash
   git clone https://github.com/yourusername/yourproject.git
   cd yourproject
```

2. **Create and activate a virtual environment:**

```bash

python -m venv myenv
source myenv/bin/activate   # On Windows use `myenv\Scripts\activate`
```

3. **Install dependencies:**

```bash

pip install -r requirements.txt
```

4. **Set up environment variables:**
   o Create a .env file based on .env.example and add your API keys and configuration.
5. **Run the application:**

```bash

python app.py
```
```

4.2 Building a Sample End-to-End Project

Building an end-to-end project means tying together all the components you've learned into a single, coherent system. In this guide, we will create a simple question-and-answer (Q&A) system that leverages a document knowledge base, an intelligent retrieval process, and a language generation pipeline—all accessible through a web interface. This project integrates data ingestion, indexing, query processing, and result generation into one complete workflow.

Project Overview

Imagine a customer support chatbot that answers user questions by searching through a repository of help documents and generating responses based on retrieved information. Our system will:

1. **Load and Index Documents:**
   Use a tool (like LlamaIndex) to ingest and index documents from a directory.
2. **Retrieve Context Based on User Query:**
   Query the index to extract relevant context for a given question.
3. **Generate Answers:**
   Use a language model pipeline (via LangChain) to generate a final response using the retrieved context.
4. **Present Results via a Web Interface:**
   Implement a simple Flask application to allow users to submit queries and view responses.

Each component is modular, making the overall system flexible and maintainable.

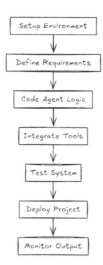

Step 1: Data Ingestion and Indexing with LlamaIndex

First, we need to load documents from a directory and create an index that will later allow us to quickly retrieve relevant information.

Code Example: Loading Documents and Building the Index

```python
python

import os
from llama_index import SimpleDirectoryReader,
GPTVectorStoreIndex

def load_documents(directory: str):
    """
    Loads text documents from the specified directory using
LlamaIndex.

    Args:
        directory (str): Path to the folder containing text
files.

    Returns:
        list: A list of document objects.
    """
    documents = SimpleDirectoryReader(directory).load_data()
    return documents

def build_index(documents):
    """
    Builds a vector store index from the provided documents.
```

```
    Args:
        documents (list): A list of document objects.

    Returns:
        GPTVectorStoreIndex: An index for efficient document
querying.
    """
    index = GPTVectorStoreIndex.from_documents(documents)
    # Save the index for persistence
    index.save_to_disk("index.json")
    return index

# Example usage:
data_directory = "data"  # Ensure your 'data' folder contains
text files
documents = load_documents(data_directory)
print(f"Loaded {len(documents)} documents.")
index = build_index(documents)
```

Commentary:

This step reads all text files in the specified folder and builds an index using vector embeddings. The index allows the system to later fetch relevant passages based on user queries.

Step 2: Query Processing and Response Generation with LangChain

Next, we set up a language generation pipeline that takes user queries, integrates retrieved context, and produces a coherent answer.

Code Example: Creating a LangChain Pipeline

```python
python

from langchain import OpenAI, LLMChain
from langchain.prompts import PromptTemplate

def create_answer_chain():
    """
    Creates a LangChain pipeline that uses a prompt template
to generate a response.

    Returns:
        LLMChain: A configured chain for answering questions.
    """
```

```python
    prompt_template = PromptTemplate(
        input_variables=["context", "question"],
        template=(
            "You are a helpful support assistant. Based on
the context provided below, "
            "answer the question as clearly as possible.\n\n"
            "Context: {context}\n"
            "Question: {question}\n"
            "Answer:"
        )
    )
    llm = OpenAI(temperature=0.7)  # Adjust parameters as
needed
    chain = LLMChain(llm=llm, prompt=prompt_template,
verbose=True)
    return chain

def retrieve_context(index, question: str) -> str:
    """
    Retrieves relevant context from the index based on the
user's question.

    Args:
        index (GPTVectorStoreIndex): The pre-built document
index.
        question (str): The user's query.

    Returns:
        str: Retrieved context.
    """
    # Query the index using the question as the search term.
    response = index.query(question)
    return response

def generate_answer(index, question: str) -> str:
    """
    Generates an answer to the user's question by retrieving
context and using the LangChain pipeline.

    Args:
        index (GPTVectorStoreIndex): The document index.
        question (str): The user's question.

    Returns:
        str: The final generated answer.
    """
    context = retrieve_context(index, question)
    chain = create_answer_chain()
    answer = chain.run(context=context, question=question)
    return answer.strip()
```

```python
# Example usage:
sample_question = "What are the key features of our new
product?"
answer = generate_answer(index, sample_question)
print("Generated Answer:\n", answer)
```

Commentary:
This pipeline sets up a prompt that includes both the retrieved context and
the user question, then sends it to an LLM to generate a detailed answer.

Step 3: Building a Web Interface with Flask

The final step is to create a web interface so that users can submit their
questions and receive answers in real time. We use Flask to build a simple
web application that integrates our indexing and answer-generation pipeline.

Code Example: Flask Application

Create a file named `app.py`:

```python
python

import os
from flask import Flask, render_template, request, jsonify
from llama_index import GPTVectorStoreIndex,
SimpleDirectoryReader
from langchain import OpenAI, LLMChain
from langchain.prompts import PromptTemplate

# Load environment variables and set API key
os.environ["OPENAI_API_KEY"] = "your_openai_api_key_here"

app = Flask(__name__)

# Load documents and build index
def load_documents(directory: str):
    return SimpleDirectoryReader(directory).load_data()

def build_index(documents):
    index = GPTVectorStoreIndex.from_documents(documents)
    index.save_to_disk("index.json")
    return index

data_directory = "data"
documents = load_documents(data_directory)
```

```python
index = build_index(documents)

# Create the LangChain answer chain
def create_answer_chain():
    prompt_template = PromptTemplate(
        input_variables=["context", "question"],
        template=(
            "You are a helpful support assistant. Based on
the context provided below, "
            "answer the question as clearly as possible.\n\n"
            "Context: {context}\n"
            "Question: {question}\n"
            "Answer:"
        )
    )
    llm = OpenAI(temperature=0.7)
    chain = LLMChain(llm=llm, prompt=prompt_template,
verbose=True)
    return chain

def retrieve_context(index, question: str) -> str:
    response = index.query(question)
    return response

def generate_answer(index, question: str) -> str:
    context = retrieve_context(index, question)
    chain = create_answer_chain()
    answer = chain.run(context=context, question=question)
    return answer.strip()

@app.route('/')
def index_page():
    return render_template('index.html')

@app.route('/ask', methods=['POST'])
def ask():
    question = request.form.get("question", "")
    answer = generate_answer(index, question)
    return jsonify({"answer": answer})

if __name__ == '__main__':
    app.run(debug=True)
```

Create a corresponding HTML template in a folder named `templates` called `index.html`:

```html
html

<!doctype html>
<html lang="en">
```

```html
<head>
    <meta charset="UTF-8">
    <title>Customer Support Q&A</title>
    <style>
        body { font-family: Arial, sans-serif; margin: 2em; }
        input, textarea { width: 100%; padding: 0.5em; }
        button { padding: 0.5em 1em; }
        #response { margin-top: 1em; background-color:
#f9f9f9; padding: 1em; border-radius: 5px; }
    </style>
</head>
<body>
    <h1>Customer Support Q&A</h1>
    <form id="questionForm">
        <textarea id="question" name="question" rows="4"
placeholder="Type your question here..."></textarea><br>
        <button type="submit">Submit</button>
    </form>
    <div id="response">
        <h2>Answer:</h2>
        <p id="answerText"></p>
    </div>
    <script src="https://code.jquery.com/jquery-
3.6.0.min.js"></script>
    <script>
        $("#questionForm").on("submit", function(event) {
            event.preventDefault();
            $.post("/ask", $(this).serialize(),
function(data) {
                $("#answerText").text(data.answer);
            });
        });
    </script>
</body>
</html>
```

Commentary:

The Flask application brings together the indexing and response generation components. When a user submits a question through the web interface, the backend processes it through our integrated pipeline and returns a detailed answer in real time.

This end-to-end project exemplifies how to build a fully functional intelligent Q&A system by integrating document ingestion, indexing, language model processing, and a user-friendly web interface. Each step is modular: loading and indexing documents with LlamaIndex, generating

112

context-aware responses using LangChain, and exposing the functionality via Flask.

By following these steps, you create a system that is adaptable to various real-world applications, whether it's customer support, internal knowledge bases, or dynamic information retrieval systems. This project not only demonstrates the practical implementation of multiple tools but also illustrates best practices in modular design, data flow management, and interface integration.

As you develop further, consider extending the system with more advanced features such as user authentication, more complex conversation handling, or integrating additional data sources. The modular approach ensures that each component can be enhanced independently, paving the way for more sophisticated and scalable autonomous systems. Enjoy the journey of transforming abstract concepts into practical, impactful solutions.

4.3 Debugging and Troubleshooting Autonomous Agents

Debugging and troubleshooting autonomous agents can be challenging due to their complex interactions, distributed components, and reliance on external services. Effective debugging requires a structured approach to identify issues, isolate components, and systematically resolve problems. This section outlines best practices and provides practical, step-by-step techniques—with detailed code examples—to help you maintain and improve your autonomous systems.

1. Establishing a Robust Logging System

A comprehensive logging system is the cornerstone of troubleshooting. It allows you to capture key events, errors, and the internal state of your agents, which can then be analyzed to identify issues.

Setting Up Python Logging

Using Python's built-in logging module, you can record informational messages, warnings, errors, and debugging details.

```python
import logging

# Configure the logging system
logging.basicConfig(
    level=logging.DEBUG,  # Set the minimum logging level
(DEBUG, INFO, WARNING, ERROR, CRITICAL)
    format="%(asctime)s [%(levelname)s] %(name)s:
%(message)s",
    handlers=[
        logging.FileHandler("agent_debug.log"),  # Write logs
to a file
        logging.StreamHandler()                  # Also output
logs to the console
    ]
)

logger = logging.getLogger("AutonomousAgent")
logger.info("Logging system initialized.")
```

Explanation:

- This configuration sets the logging level to DEBUG so that all messages are recorded.
- Logs are both saved to a file and printed to the console, which is useful during development and for post-mortem analysis.

---

2. Implementing Error Handling in Agent Functions

Each autonomous agent should have built-in error handling to catch exceptions and log meaningful error messages. Using try/except blocks enables you to isolate issues within individual modules.

Example: Error Handling in a Query Processing Agent

```python
def process_query(query: str) -> str:
    """
    Processes a user query using an LLM and returns a
response.

    Args:
        query (str): The input query from the user.
```

114

```
    Returns:
        str: The response from the language model.
    """
    try:
        # Simulate a call to an LLM service (e.g., OpenAI's
API)
        response = openai.Completion.create(
            engine="text-davinci-003",
            prompt=f"Answer the following question: {query}",
            max_tokens=150,
            temperature=0.7
        )
        answer = response.choices[0].text.strip()
        logger.info("Query processed successfully.")
        return answer
    except Exception as e:
        logger.error(f"Error processing query: {e}",
exc_info=True)
        return "Sorry, an error occurred while processing
your query."
```

Explanation:

- The try block attempts to process the query.
- If an exception occurs, the error is logged with `exc_info=True` to include the traceback, aiding in debugging.
- A fallback message is returned, ensuring the system remains responsive.

---

3. Using Unit Tests to Isolate Issues

Unit tests allow you to verify that individual components behave as expected. Using a framework like `unittest` or `pytest`, you can write tests to cover key functionalities of your agents.

Example: Unit Testing an Agent's Functionality

```python
import unittest

class TestAgentFunctions(unittest.TestCase):
    def test_process_query_success(self):
        # Test with a normal query input
```

```
        query = "What is the capital of France?"
        response = process_query(query)
        self.assertTrue(len(response) > 0)

    def test_process_query_failure(self):
        # Simulate an error by providing invalid parameters
        # Here we override openai.Completion.create
temporarily to raise an exception
        original_function = openai.Completion.create
        openai.Completion.create = lambda **kwargs: (_ for _
in ()).throw(Exception("Simulated error"))

        query = "This will trigger an error"
        response = process_query(query)
        self.assertEqual(response, "Sorry, an error occurred
while processing your query.")

        # Restore the original function
        openai.Completion.create = original_function

if __name__ == '__main__':
    unittest.main()
```

Explanation:

- This test suite checks that the agent returns a valid response for a normal query and gracefully handles errors when an exception is raised.
- Temporarily overriding the function simulates an error scenario, allowing you to verify that error handling works as expected.

---

4. Implementing Monitoring and Real-Time Diagnostics

In production, real-time monitoring can alert you to issues as they occur. Integrating tools like Prometheus or using cloud-based monitoring services can provide insights into performance, error rates, and resource usage. Here's a conceptual example using Flask's built-in route to check system health.

Example: Health Check Endpoint

```python
@app.route('/health', methods=['GET'])
```

```
def health_check():
    """
    Provides a simple health check endpoint to monitor system
status.
    """
    try:
        # Perform simple diagnostic checks (e.g., verifying
memory or service status)
        status = {
            "status": "healthy",
            "message": "All systems are functioning
normally."
        }
        logger.info("Health check passed.")
        return jsonify(status), 200
    except Exception as e:
        logger.error(f"Health check failed: {e}",
exc_info=True)
        return jsonify({"status": "unhealthy", "message":
"There is a problem with the system."}), 500
```

Explanation:

- This endpoint can be polled by a monitoring system to ensure that the application is running correctly.
- Logging within the endpoint helps trace any intermittent issues that might not trigger a complete failure.

---

5. Practical Debugging Tips and Best Practices

- **Isolate Components:** Test individual modules separately to identify the source of issues.
- **Incremental Development:** Build your system in small, testable increments. Regularly commit changes and run tests.
- **Error Reporting:** Implement robust error reporting that includes both user-friendly messages and detailed logs.
- **Automated Testing:** Integrate automated tests into your CI/CD pipeline to catch errors early.
- **Use Debuggers:** Tools like `pdb` in Python can be invaluable for stepping through code when issues arise.
- **Monitor Performance:** Regularly review logs and performance metrics to catch anomalies that may indicate deeper problems.

Personal Note:
During development, I've found that combining thorough logging with a disciplined unit testing approach saves significant time. Debugging becomes a systematic process rather than a hunt for elusive bugs.

Debugging and troubleshooting are essential practices in the development of autonomous agents. By establishing robust logging, implementing targeted error handling, writing comprehensive unit tests, and integrating real-time monitoring, you can significantly reduce downtime and improve system reliability. These techniques, illustrated with practical code examples, provide a framework that you can adapt to any autonomous system you build. As you continue developing your projects, remember that each debugging session is an opportunity to learn more about your system's behavior and to improve its resilience in the face of real-world challenges.

Chapter 5: Advanced Topics and Best Practices

As your autonomous systems evolve from prototypes to production-ready solutions, addressing advanced topics becomes essential. This chapter covers key areas that will elevate your projects to a higher level of reliability, efficiency, and ethical responsibility. We explore security and privacy, scalability and performance, testing and continuous improvement, API integration, and ethical governance. Each section is designed to provide clear insights and best practices that you can apply to your projects.

5.1 Security and Privacy in Agent Systems

Security and privacy are critical aspects of autonomous agent systems, especially when these systems interact with sensitive data or perform high-stakes tasks. Ensuring that your agents operate securely and respect user privacy is not only a technical requirement but also a cornerstone for building user trust and complying with legal regulations. This section outlines a step-by-step approach to implement robust security measures, with practical code examples to illustrate each concept.

1. Implementing Secure Data Storage and Transmission

Step 1: Encrypting Sensitive Data

When storing or transmitting sensitive data, encryption is essential. Python's `cryptography` library provides a straightforward way to encrypt and decrypt data.

Installation:

```bash
pip install cryptography
```

Example: Encrypting and Decrypting Data

```python
from cryptography.fernet import Fernet

# Generate a key (do this once and store it securely)
def generate_key():
    key = Fernet.generate_key()
    with open("secret.key", "wb") as key_file:
        key_file.write(key)
    return key

# Load the key from the file
def load_key():
    return open("secret.key", "rb").read()

# Encrypt data
def encrypt_data(data: str, key: bytes) -> bytes:
    f = Fernet(key)
    encrypted = f.encrypt(data.encode())
    return encrypted

# Decrypt data
def decrypt_data(encrypted_data: bytes, key: bytes) -> str:
    f = Fernet(key)
    decrypted = f.decrypt(encrypted_data).decode()
    return decrypted

# Usage example
if not os.path.exists("secret.key"):
    generate_key()
key = load_key()
original_data = "Sensitive agent configuration data."
encrypted = encrypt_data(original_data, key)
print("Encrypted Data:", encrypted)
decrypted = decrypt_data(encrypted, key)
print("Decrypted Data:", decrypted)
```

Explanation:

- **Key Generation and Storage:** A symmetric key is generated and saved to a file, then loaded when needed.
- **Encryption and Decryption:** Data is encrypted before storage or transmission and decrypted when accessed, ensuring sensitive information remains secure.

2. Secure API Communication

When autonomous agents interact with external services or each other, ensure that communications are secure.

Step 1: Using HTTPS for API Requests

Python's `requests` library supports HTTPS out of the box. Always verify SSL certificates to prevent man-in-the-middle attacks.

Example: Secure API Call

```python
import requests

def fetch_secure_data(api_url: str) -> dict:
    try:
        response = requests.get(api_url, verify=True,
timeout=10)
        response.raise_for_status()  # Raises HTTPError for
bad responses
        return response.json()
    except requests.RequestException as e:
        print(f"API request error: {e}")
        return {}

# Usage example (ensure the API URL uses HTTPS)
api_url = "https://api.example.com/data"
data = fetch_secure_data(api_url)
print("Secure API Data:", data)
```

Explanation:

- **HTTPS Verification:** The `verify=True` parameter ensures that SSL certificates are checked.
- **Timeout and Error Handling:** Using a timeout and proper error handling prevents the system from hanging or leaking sensitive error details.

3. Implementing Access Control

Controlling who can access your autonomous agents and their data is vital for security.

Step 1: Using Environment Variables for API Keys

Storing sensitive keys in environment variables keeps them out of your source code. Using the `python-dotenv` package helps manage these variables.

Installation:

```bash
pip install python-dotenv
```

Example: Loading Environment Variables

```python
import os
from dotenv import load_dotenv

# Load environment variables from a .env file
load_dotenv()

# Access the API key securely
api_key = os.getenv("OPENAI_API_KEY")
print("Loaded API Key:", api_key)
```

Explanation:

- **Environment Variables:** They provide a secure way to manage secrets without hardcoding them.
- **python-dotenv:** This package automatically loads variables from a `.env` file, streamlining configuration across environments.

Step 2: Role-Based Access Control (RBAC)

For systems with multiple users or components, implementing RBAC ensures that each entity only accesses what it's authorized to.

Conceptual Approach:

122

- **Define Roles:** Identify roles such as "admin", "developer", or "user".
- **Assign Permissions:** Each role has specific permissions. For example, only admins can modify system configurations.
- **Enforce in Code:** When an API call is made, check the user's role and allow or deny access accordingly.

Example Pseudocode for RBAC:

```python
def check_access(user_role: str, required_role: str) -> bool:
    role_hierarchy = {"user": 1, "developer": 2, "admin": 3}
    return role_hierarchy.get(user_role, 0) >= role_hierarchy.get(required_role, 0)

# Example usage:
user_role = "developer"
if check_access(user_role, "admin"):
    print("Access granted.")
else:
    print("Access denied.")
```

Explanation:

- **Role Hierarchy:** A simple dictionary assigns numerical values to roles.
- **Access Check:** The function compares roles to determine if access should be granted.

---

4. Monitoring and Auditing

Proactive monitoring and regular auditing are crucial for maintaining security and privacy over time.

Step 1: Logging Sensitive Events

Integrate logging to monitor system activity, such as user actions, data access, and error occurrences.

Example: Python Logging for Security Events

```python
```

```
import logging

# Configure logging
logging.basicConfig(
    level=logging.INFO,
    format="%(asctime)s [%(levelname)s] %(message)s",
    handlers=[logging.FileHandler("security.log"),
logging.StreamHandler()]
)

def log_event(event: str):
    logging.info(event)

# Log a security event
log_event("User 'admin' accessed sensitive configuration
data.")
```

Explanation:

- **Logging Configuration:** Logs are recorded with timestamps and severity levels, both to a file and to the console.
- **Event Logging:** Regular logging of security-relevant events creates an audit trail that can be reviewed during audits.

Step 2: Integrating Real-Time Monitoring

Use tools like Prometheus or cloud-based monitoring solutions (e.g., AWS CloudWatch) to keep track of system health, performance metrics, and potential security incidents. While full integration is beyond this example, the basic idea is to expose relevant metrics through an API endpoint and configure a monitoring system to alert you when anomalies occur.

5. Data Privacy Considerations

Ensuring data privacy involves both technical measures and adherence to legal standards.

Key Practices:

- **Data Anonymization:** Remove or obfuscate personal identifiers from data used for training or analytics.

- **Consent Management:** Implement clear mechanisms for users to give or revoke consent for data collection and usage.
- **Compliance:** Adhere to regulations like GDPR or HIPAA by implementing data minimization, secure data deletion, and transparency in data usage policies.

Example Strategy (Conceptual):

- **Anonymization Function:** Create a function that strips personal information from data before processing.
- **User Consent Check:** Verify user consent at the point of data ingestion, and log consent status for audit purposes.

Implementing robust security and privacy measures in autonomous agent systems is not an optional extra—it is an essential part of the development process. By following these best practices—encrypting sensitive data, ensuring secure communication, implementing access control, and integrating comprehensive monitoring and logging—you build a strong foundation that protects both your system and its users.

The code examples provided here demonstrate practical approaches to securing your application. From encrypting data to verifying API communications and enforcing role-based access, each step contributes to a secure and trustworthy environment. As you scale your system and integrate more components, maintaining a focus on security and privacy will help prevent vulnerabilities and ensure compliance with legal and ethical standards.

These practices, when combined with a proactive approach to monitoring and regular auditing, form a robust security framework that safeguards your autonomous agents in real-world applications. Embracing these strategies will not only enhance your system's resilience but also build user trust, which is paramount in today's data-driven landscape.

5.2 Scalability and Performance Optimization

Scalability and performance optimization are crucial when building autonomous systems that must handle increasing workloads and operate reliably under varied conditions. By designing your system to scale horizontally and optimizing its performance at every layer, you can ensure that your solution remains responsive and efficient as demands grow. This guide outlines practical strategies—from profiling and caching to leveraging concurrency and distributed processing—with step-by-step explanations and complete code examples.

---

1. Profiling Your Application

Before optimizing, it's important to identify bottlenecks using profiling tools. Python's built-in `cProfile` module provides an easy way to measure the performance of your code.

Step-by-Step: Using cProfile

```python
python

import cProfile
import pstats

def compute_heavy_task(n):
    total = 0
    for i in range(n):
        total += i ** 2
    return total

def main():
    result = compute_heavy_task(100000)
    print("Result:", result)

if __name__ == "__main__":
    profiler = cProfile.Profile()
    profiler.enable()
    main()
    profiler.disable()
    stats = pstats.Stats(profiler).sort_stats("cumtime")
    stats.print_stats(10)
```

Explanation:

- The `compute_heavy_task` function simulates a resource-intensive operation.
- The profiler wraps the `main` function to record performance data, which is then printed sorted by cumulative time.

- Use these insights to identify functions that require optimization.

---

2. Caching Strategies

Caching stores the results of expensive function calls and reuses them when the same inputs occur again, reducing redundant computations.

Step-by-Step: Using `functools.lru_cache`

```python
python

from functools import lru_cache
import time

@lru_cache(maxsize=128)
def expensive_calculation(n):
    time.sleep(2)  # Simulate a time-consuming task
    return n * n

def main():
    start = time.time()
    print("First call:", expensive_calculation(10))  # Takes
~2 seconds
    print("Second call:", expensive_calculation(10))  #
Returns instantly from cache
    end = time.time()
    print(f"Time elapsed: {end - start:.2f} seconds")

if __name__ == "__main__":
    main()
```

Explanation:

- The `expensive_calculation` function simulates a heavy computation.
- The `lru_cache` decorator caches results, so subsequent calls with the same argument are fast.
- This technique is useful when you have repeated calculations with identical inputs.

---

3. Concurrency and Parallelism

Leveraging concurrency allows your application to handle multiple tasks simultaneously, improving throughput and reducing wait times.

Step-by-Step: Using `asyncio` for Asynchronous I/O

```python
python

import asyncio
import aiohttp

async def fetch_url(session, url):
    async with session.get(url) as response:
        return await response.text()

async def main():
    urls = [
        "https://httpbin.org/delay/2",
        "https://httpbin.org/delay/2",
        "https://httpbin.org/delay/2"
    ]
    async with aiohttp.ClientSession() as session:
        tasks = [fetch_url(session, url) for url in urls]
        responses = await asyncio.gather(*tasks)
        for i, text in enumerate(responses):
            print(f"Response {i+1} length: {len(text)}")

if __name__ == "__main__":
    asyncio.run(main())
```

Explanation:

- `aiohttp` is used to make asynchronous HTTP requests.
- `asyncio.gather` runs multiple requests concurrently, significantly reducing total runtime compared to sequential requests.

Step-by-Step: Using `multiprocessing` for CPU-bound Tasks

```python
python

from multiprocessing import Pool
import time

def compute_square(n):
    time.sleep(1)  # Simulate a CPU-bound operation
    return n * n
```

128

```
def main():
    numbers = [1, 2, 3, 4, 5]
    with Pool(5) as pool:
        results = pool.map(compute_square, numbers)
    print("Results:", results)

if __name__ == "__main__":
    main()
```

Explanation:

- The `multiprocessing.Pool` module allows CPU-bound tasks to run in parallel across multiple processes.
- This can reduce the total processing time by utilizing multiple cores.

---

4. Load Balancing and Distributed Processing

For large-scale systems, distributing workloads across multiple servers or nodes ensures that no single component becomes a bottleneck.

Step-by-Step: Using Celery for Distributed Task Queue

1. **Install Celery and Redis:**

```bash
pip install celery redis
```

2. **Create a Celery Task File (`tasks.py`):**

```python
from celery import Celery
import time

app = Celery('tasks', broker='redis://localhost:6379/0')

@app.task
def process_data(n):
    time.sleep(2)   # Simulate processing time
    return n * n
```

3. **Dispatch Tasks from a Script:**

129

```python
from tasks import process_data

def main():
    tasks = [process_data.delay(i) for i in range(10)]
    results = [task.get(timeout=10) for task in tasks]
    print("Celery Results:", results)

if __name__ == "__main__":
    main()
```

Explanation:

- Celery distributes tasks across workers, with Redis as the message broker.
- This setup allows you to scale processing by simply adding more worker nodes.

5. Optimizing Data Flow

Efficient data handling is critical for performance. Asynchronous processing and careful data transformation can reduce latency and improve throughput.

Step-by-Step: Using Asynchronous File I/O with `aiofiles`

```python
import asyncio
import aiofiles

async def read_file(file_path):
    async with aiofiles.open(file_path, mode='r') as file:
        contents = await file.read()
    return contents

async def main():
    file_path = "large_text_file.txt"
    contents = await read_file(file_path)
    print(f"File length: {len(contents)} characters")

if __name__ == "__main__":
    asyncio.run(main())
```

Explanation:

- Asynchronous file I/O allows your application to handle other tasks while waiting for file operations to complete, which is especially useful when dealing with large datasets.

Scalability and performance optimization are about designing your system to handle increased load and operate efficiently under diverse conditions. Through profiling, caching, concurrency, and distributed processing, you can build a system that not only meets current requirements but also scales gracefully with future demands.

Each step—from using cProfile to identify bottlenecks to implementing caching strategies, leveraging asynchronous operations, and distributing tasks with Celery—provides a building block for a high-performance system. By integrating these practices into your development process, you create a robust, efficient, and scalable architecture capable of supporting sophisticated autonomous agents.

The code examples provided here are practical and ready for implementation, giving you the tools to experiment, measure performance, and optimize as needed. As you build and refine your system, remember that scalability and performance optimization are continuous processes, requiring regular monitoring, testing, and adaptation to evolving workloads. Enjoy the process of making your systems faster and more efficient, and watch as your intelligent solutions perform reliably even under heavy load.

5.3 Testing, Quality Assurance, and Continuous Improvement

Testing, quality assurance, and continuous improvement form the backbone of building reliable autonomous agent systems. They ensure that each component performs as expected, that integration across modules is smooth, and that the system evolves over time while maintaining high standards. This guide explains a structured approach to implementing tests at various levels, automating quality checks, and embedding a culture of continuous improvement into your development workflow.

1. Unit Testing

Unit tests verify the behavior of individual functions or classes in isolation. By testing small, independent components, you catch errors early and ensure that each piece works correctly.

Step-by-Step: Writing Unit Tests with Python's unittest

Consider an autonomous agent function that processes user queries. Here's how you can write unit tests for it.

Agent Function Example

```python
python

def process_query(query: str) -> str:
    """
    Processes a user query using a simple transformation.

    Args:
        query (str): The user's input query.

    Returns:
        str: A processed response.
    """
    # For demonstration, convert the query to uppercase.
    if not query:
        raise ValueError("Query cannot be empty.")
    return query.upper()
```

Writing Unit Tests

Create a file named `test_agent.py` and add the following tests:

```python
python

import unittest
from agent_module import process_query  # Assume the function is in agent_module.py

class TestProcessQuery(unittest.TestCase):
    def test_process_query_normal(self):
        query = "How is the weather today?"
        expected = "HOW IS THE WEATHER TODAY?"
        result = process_query(query)
        self.assertEqual(result, expected)
```

```python
    def test_process_query_empty(self):
        with self.assertRaises(ValueError):
            process_query("")

if __name__ == "__main__":
    unittest.main()
```

Explanation:

- The first test checks that a typical query is transformed correctly.
- The second test verifies that an empty query raises a ValueError.
- Running `python test_agent.py` will execute these tests and report results.

---

2. Integration Testing

Integration tests ensure that multiple components work together as intended. In an autonomous system, this might involve testing the interaction between a query processing module and a response generator.

Step-by-Step: Integration Testing Example

Suppose you have two functions: one for retrieving context from an index and another for generating a response using a language model. Their integration can be tested as follows:

Example Functions

```python
def retrieve_context(query: str) -> str:
    """
    Simulates retrieving context based on a query.
    For this example, simply returns a fixed string.
    """
    return "This is the retrieved context for the query."

def generate_response(context: str, query: str) -> str:
    """
    Simulates generating a response using the provided
context and query.
    For this example, combines the context and query.
    """
```

```
    if not context or not query:
        raise ValueError("Context and query must be
provided.")
    return f"Response based on '{context}' and the query
'{query}'."
```

Integration Test

Create a file named `test_integration.py`:

```python
import unittest
from agent_module import retrieve_context, generate_response

class TestIntegration(unittest.TestCase):
    def test_full_workflow(self):
        query = "What is the impact of AI?"
        context = retrieve_context(query)
        response = generate_response(context, query)
        expected = f"Response based on '{context}' and the
query '{query}'."
        self.assertEqual(response, expected)

if __name__ == "__main__":
    unittest.main()
```

Explanation:

- This test simulates a complete workflow by retrieving context and then generating a response.
- It confirms that the integrated system produces the expected output.

---

3. End-to-End Testing

End-to-end (E2E) tests simulate real-world usage scenarios by testing the entire application, including the user interface. For web-based autonomous systems, tools like Selenium or Flask's test client can be useful.

Step-by-Step: E2E Testing with Flask's Test Client

Assume you have a Flask application (`app.py`) that provides an endpoint for processing queries. You can test it end-to-end as follows:

Flask App Example (Simplified)

```python
from flask import Flask, request, jsonify

app = Flask(__name__)

@app.route('/process', methods=['POST'])
def process():
    query = request.form.get("query", "")
    if not query:
        return jsonify({"error": "No query provided"}), 400
    # For this example, simply echo the query in uppercase.
    return jsonify({"response": query.upper()})

if __name__ == "__main__":
    app.run(debug=True)
```

E2E Test Using Flask Test Client

Create a file named test_app.py:

```python
import unittest
from app import app

class TestFlaskApp(unittest.TestCase):
    def setUp(self):
        self.app = app.test_client()
        self.app.testing = True

    def test_process_endpoint_success(self):
        response = self.app.post('/process', data={'query':
'hello world'})
        self.assertEqual(response.status_code, 200)
        data = response.get_json()
        self.assertEqual(data["response"], "HELLO WORLD")

    def test_process_endpoint_failure(self):
        response = self.app.post('/process', data={'query':
''})
        self.assertEqual(response.status_code, 400)
        data = response.get_json()
        self.assertIn("error", data)

if __name__ == "__main__":
    unittest.main()
```

Explanation:

- `setUp()` creates a test client for the Flask app.
- Tests cover both successful processing and failure when no query is provided.
- Running these tests verifies that the endpoint works as expected.

---

4. Continuous Integration and Quality Assurance

Integrating automated tests into a CI/CD pipeline ensures that your code remains reliable with every change. Tools like GitHub Actions, Travis CI, or Jenkins can automatically run your tests on each commit.

Step-by-Step: GitHub Actions Workflow Example

Create a file `.github/workflows/ci.yml` in your repository:

```yaml
yaml

name: CI

on: [push, pull_request]

jobs:
  build:
    runs-on: ubuntu-latest

    steps:
    - name: Checkout repository
      uses: actions/checkout@v2

    - name: Set up Python 3.8
      uses: actions/setup-python@v2
      with:
        python-version: '3.8'

    - name: Install dependencies
      run: |
        python -m pip install --upgrade pip
        pip install -r requirements.txt

    - name: Run unit tests
      run: |
        python -m unittest discover -s tests
```

Explanation:

- This GitHub Actions workflow runs on every push or pull request.
- It checks out the code, sets up Python, installs dependencies, and runs tests located in a `tests` directory.
- Integrating such workflows helps catch issues early and maintain code quality continuously.

---

5. Continuous Improvement and Monitoring

Testing isn't a one-time effort—it's an ongoing process. As your system evolves, so should your tests. Regularly update your test cases to cover new features and edge cases. In addition, implement monitoring to track application performance and detect anomalies in production.

Best Practices for Continuous Improvement

- **Regular Code Reviews:**
  Conduct code reviews to catch issues early and share best practices across the team.
- **Automated Test Coverage:**
  Ensure that most of your code is covered by tests. Tools like `coverage.py` can help track this.
- **Monitoring and Feedback:**
  Use logging and performance monitoring tools to gather real-time data on system performance, and incorporate user feedback to continuously refine your system.

Personal Note:
In my experience, integrating testing into every phase of development not only prevents bugs but also fosters a culture of continuous learning and improvement, which is essential for long-term project success.

Testing, quality assurance, and continuous improvement are integral to the development of autonomous agent systems. By writing unit, integration, and end-to-end tests, you create a safety net that catches errors early and ensures your system behaves as expected. Automating these tests within a CI/CD pipeline further enhances your workflow by providing immediate feedback on code changes.

5.4 Integrating External APIs and Data Sources

Integrating external APIs and data sources is a critical part of building intelligent systems that can leverage real-world information in real time. This guide explains how to set up API integrations, manage authentication, handle data responses, and combine multiple sources into your autonomous agent ecosystem. The following sections provide step-by-step instructions along with code examples that you can implement directly in your projects.

1. Understanding API Integration

External APIs allow your system to access services and data hosted by other providers. Whether it's retrieving weather data, stock prices, or even social media feeds, APIs serve as bridges between your application and external information sources. A robust integration involves:

- **Authentication:** Securely connecting to the API using methods such as API keys, OAuth, or tokens.
- **Data Request:** Sending requests to the API endpoints using standardized protocols (usually HTTP/HTTPS).
- **Response Handling:** Parsing and processing the returned data (typically in JSON or XML format).
- **Error Handling:** Managing API failures, rate limits, or unexpected data formats to ensure your system remains stable.

2. Setting Up Your Environment for API Integration

Before writing the integration code, ensure that you have the necessary libraries installed. For most RESTful API interactions, the `requests` library is sufficient.

Installation

```bash
bash

pip install requests python-dotenv
```

Explanation:

- **requests:** Handles HTTP requests easily.
- **python-dotenv:** Manages environment variables securely.

Create a `.env` file to store your API credentials:

```
# .env file
API_KEY=your_api_key_here
Load these variables in your Python code:
python
Copy
import os
from dotenv import load_dotenv

# Load environment variables from .env file
load_dotenv()
API_KEY = os.getenv("API_KEY")
print("Loaded API Key:", API_KEY)
```

3. Making a Basic API Request

A fundamental example of API integration is fetching data from a simple endpoint. Consider the following example using a public API to retrieve user information.

Code Example: GET Request with Error Handling

```python
python

import requests

def fetch_user_data(user_id: int) -> dict:
    """
    Fetches user data from a sample API endpoint.

    Args:
        user_id (int): The ID of the user.

    Returns:
        dict: Parsed JSON response containing user data.
    """
```

```python
    url =
f"https://jsonplaceholder.typicode.com/users/{user_id}"
    try:
        response = requests.get(url, timeout=5)
        response.raise_for_status()   # Raises an HTTPError if
the HTTP request returned an unsuccessful status code
        user_data = response.json()
        return user_data
    except requests.RequestException as e:
        print(f"Error fetching user data: {e}")
        return {}

# Example usage
user_info = fetch_user_data(1)
print("User Data:", user_info)
```

Explanation:

- The function constructs a URL with the given user ID and makes an HTTP GET request.
- Error handling ensures that any issues (like timeouts or network errors) are caught and logged.
- The JSON response is parsed into a Python dictionary for further use.

---

4. Integrating a Complex External API

For more sophisticated integrations, such as accessing financial data or weather information, you may need to manage authentication and additional parameters. Let's use the OpenWeatherMap API as an example.

Step-by-Step: OpenWeatherMap API Integration

1. **Sign Up and Get Your API Key:**
   Register on the OpenWeatherMap website and obtain an API key.
2. **Set Up Environment Variables:**
   Store your API key in the .env file as shown earlier.
3. **Make an API Call:**
   Retrieve current weather data for a specific city.

Code Example: Fetching Weather Data

```python
```

```python
import requests
import os
from dotenv import load_dotenv

load_dotenv()
WEATHER_API_KEY = os.getenv("OPENWEATHER_API_KEY")  # Add
your key to .env

def fetch_weather(city: str) -> dict:
    """
    Fetches current weather data for a given city from
OpenWeatherMap.

    Args:
        city (str): The name of the city.

    Returns:
        dict: Weather data as a dictionary.
    """
    base_url =
"https://api.openweathermap.org/data/2.5/weather"
    params = {
        "q": city,
        "appid": WEATHER_API_KEY,
        "units": "metric"  # Use metric units for temperature
    }
    try:
        response = requests.get(base_url, params=params,
timeout=5)
        response.raise_for_status()
        weather_data = response.json()
        return weather_data
    except requests.RequestException as e:
        print(f"Error fetching weather data: {e}")
        return {}

# Example usage:
city_weather = fetch_weather("London")
print("Weather Data for London:", city_weather)
```

Explanation:

- **Parameterization:** The API key and city name are passed as parameters, ensuring flexibility.
- **Units:** Specifying units (e.g., metric) makes the data more user-friendly.
- **Error Handling:** Similar error handling as in previous examples ensures robustness.

5. Combining Multiple API Data Sources

Autonomous systems often benefit from integrating data from multiple APIs. For example, you could combine weather data with geographical data to build a comprehensive travel assistant.

Step-by-Step: Merging Data from Two APIs

Let's say we have:

- The OpenWeatherMap API for weather data.
- A Geocoding API to convert city names to coordinates (e.g., OpenCage Geocoder).

Code Example: Combining Weather and Geocoding Data

```python
python

def fetch_geocode(city: str) -> dict:
    """
    Fetches geocoding data for a given city using the
OpenCage Geocoder API.

    Args:
        city (str): The name of the city.

    Returns:
        dict: Geocoding data containing latitude and
longitude.
    """
    GEOCODE_API_KEY = os.getenv("OPENCAGE_API_KEY")   # Add
this key to your .env file
    base_url = "https://api.opencagedata.com/geocode/v1/json"
    params = {
        "q": city,
        "key": GEOCODE_API_KEY,
        "limit": 1
    }
    try:
        response = requests.get(base_url, params=params,
timeout=5)
        response.raise_for_status()
        geocode_data = response.json()
        if geocode_data["results"]:
            return geocode_data["results"][0]["geometry"]
```

```python
        else:
            return {}
    except requests.RequestException as e:
        print(f"Error fetching geocode data: {e}")
        return {}

def get_travel_info(city: str) -> dict:
    """
    Combines weather and geocoding data to provide travel
information for a city.

    Args:
        city (str): The name of the city.

    Returns:
        dict: A combined dictionary with weather and location
data.
    """
    weather = fetch_weather(city)
    geocode = fetch_geocode(city)
    travel_info = {
        "city": city,
        "weather": weather,
        "location": geocode
    }
    return travel_info

# Example usage:
travel_info_london = get_travel_info("London")
print("Travel Info for London:", travel_info_london)
```

Explanation:

- **fetch_geocode:** Retrieves the latitude and longitude for the specified city.
- **get_travel_info:** Combines the geocoding data with weather data, offering a richer dataset.
- This pattern of merging responses from multiple APIs is common in real-world applications, where diverse data sources must be synthesized to provide valuable insights.

6. Best Practices for API Integration

- **Standardize Data Formats:**
  Convert data to common formats (e.g., JSON) to ensure consistency across your system.
- **Handle Rate Limits and Quotas:**
  Implement retry mechanisms and monitor API usage to avoid exceeding rate limits.
- **Secure API Keys:**
  Use environment variables or secret management tools to protect your credentials.
- **Error and Exception Handling:**
  Always check for error responses and include fallback mechanisms for graceful degradation.
- **Documentation and Testing:**
  Maintain clear documentation for each API integration and develop tests that verify data accuracy and response handling.

Integrating external APIs and data sources extends the capabilities of your autonomous systems by enabling access to real-time, diverse data. The step-by-step examples above—from basic API calls with secure error handling to combining multiple data sources—demonstrate practical implementations that can be directly applied in real-world projects. Each code example is designed to be easily adapted and extended to suit your particular use case.

By following these guidelines and best practices, you can build robust integrations that enhance your system's functionality and provide valuable insights to your users. As your project evolves, consider expanding these integrations, optimizing data flow, and automating error handling to create a resilient, scalable ecosystem. Enjoy the process of integrating external data—it's a powerful way to enrich your autonomous agents and bring them closer to real-world applications.

5.5 Ethical Implications and Governance Strategies

Ethical implications and governance strategies are not mere afterthoughts—they are fundamental to developing autonomous systems that are responsible, transparent, and trusted by users. As these systems become more pervasive and influential, addressing ethical concerns and establishing robust governance frameworks is essential for both legal compliance and maintaining public confidence. This guide outlines practical insights and expert perspectives on how to design, implement, and monitor ethical and governance measures within your autonomous agent systems.

Ethical Implications: Understanding and Mitigating Bias

Autonomous agents often rely on data-driven models, and these models can inadvertently propagate biases present in their training data. One of the first steps in addressing ethical concerns is recognizing that bias can manifest in various forms—from gender and racial biases to socioeconomic and cultural assumptions.

Key Strategies for Bias Mitigation:

- **Data Auditing:**
  Regularly audit your data sources to identify potential biases. This involves analyzing datasets for representation gaps and skewed distributions that might influence the behavior of your models.
- **Diverse Data Sourcing:**
  Incorporate diverse data sources that represent a broad range of perspectives. This can help reduce the risk of reinforcing a narrow worldview in your autonomous systems.
- **Algorithmic Fairness Techniques:**
  Implement fairness-aware algorithms that adjust for bias during the training phase. Techniques such as re-weighting or adversarial debiasing can help ensure that outputs are more balanced.
- **Transparent Reporting:**
  Document the steps taken to mitigate bias and provide transparency in how decisions are made. This builds trust with users and stakeholders by showing that ethical considerations are integral to the development process.

Governance Strategies: Ensuring Accountability and Transparency

A well-governed system is one where roles, responsibilities, and decision-making processes are clearly defined and transparent. Governance in the context of autonomous agents involves creating policies, standards, and oversight mechanisms that guide the system throughout its lifecycle.

Key Components of Effective Governance:

- **Clear Accountability Structures:**
  Define who is responsible for what aspects of the system—from data management to algorithmic decisions. This might involve setting up an internal oversight committee or appointing dedicated roles (e.g., Chief Ethics Officer) to monitor system behavior.
- **Explainability and Transparency:**
  Develop systems that can explain their decision-making processes. Explainable AI (XAI) techniques are crucial for providing insights into how and why an agent arrived at a particular decision. This transparency is vital for both internal audits and external regulatory compliance.
- **Regular Audits and Reviews:**
  Establish a schedule for regular audits of your autonomous systems. These audits should evaluate not only performance and accuracy but also ethical compliance and bias mitigation measures. Third-party audits can provide an additional layer of credibility.
- **Compliance with Legal Frameworks:**
  Ensure that your system adheres to relevant laws and regulations, such as GDPR for data protection or HIPAA for healthcare applications. This involves not only implementing technical safeguards but also maintaining proper documentation and processes for data handling.
- **Stakeholder Engagement:**
  Engage with a broad range of stakeholders—including end users, domain experts, and regulatory bodies—to gather feedback and continuously refine your governance framework. This collaborative approach ensures that the system aligns with societal values and addresses the needs of all parties involved.

Integrating Ethical and Governance Measures into the Development Process

Embedding ethical considerations and governance strategies into your system's architecture requires a proactive approach from the very beginning of the development process. Rather than treating these aspects as add-ons, they should be integrated into every stage of design, implementation, and deployment.

Practical Implementation Steps:

- **Design for Privacy:**
  Incorporate privacy-by-design principles. For example, use data anonymization techniques to protect user identities and implement strict access controls from the outset.
- **Transparent Documentation:**
  Maintain clear documentation of data sources, model decisions, and governance policies. This documentation serves as both an internal guideline and a public record, demonstrating your commitment to ethical practices.
- **Iterative Feedback Loops:**
  Establish mechanisms for continuous feedback from users and stakeholders. Regularly update your models and governance policies based on this feedback, ensuring that the system evolves responsibly over time.
- **Automated Monitoring and Reporting:**
  Use automated tools to monitor system performance and flag potential ethical or governance issues in real time. Alerts and dashboards can help you quickly address concerns before they escalate.
- **Training and Awareness:**
  Educate your development team on the importance of ethical AI and governance. Regular training sessions can help ensure that everyone involved understands the potential risks and is equipped to mitigate them.

Expert Commentary

Experts in the field emphasize that ethical AI is not just about avoiding harm; it's about actively promoting fairness, accountability, and transparency. By incorporating rigorous governance frameworks and ethical guidelines into your system, you build trust with users and create a sustainable foundation for innovation. One leading researcher noted that "a truly intelligent system is one that can explain its decisions and evolve responsibly in a complex, real-world environment." This perspective highlights the necessity of aligning technological advances with ethical considerations to ensure that autonomous systems benefit society as a whole.

Incorporating ethical implications and governance strategies into your autonomous agent systems is a multifaceted challenge that requires careful planning, continuous monitoring, and a commitment to transparency. By focusing on bias mitigation, clear accountability, regulatory compliance, and stakeholder engagement, you create a robust framework that not only protects users and data but also enhances the credibility and effectiveness of your systems.

This integrated approach is essential for developing intelligent systems that are not only powerful and efficient but also socially responsible and trustworthy. Embracing these principles from the outset will help you build systems that can adapt to evolving legal, ethical, and societal standards, ensuring long-term success and positive impact in the rapidly changing world of AI.

Chapter 6: Deployment, Monitoring, and Maintenance

Successfully deploying an autonomous agent system marks the transition from development to production, but it's only the beginning. Once your system is live, you need to ensure it runs smoothly, scales to meet demand, and remains secure over time. This chapter explains strategies for deploying agents in both cloud and on-premises environments, establishing robust CI/CD pipelines, and implementing comprehensive monitoring, logging, and maintenance practices. The goal is to create a system that is resilient, scalable, and easy to update as your needs evolve.

6.1 Deploying AI Agents in Cloud and On-Premises Environments

Deploying AI agents in both cloud and on-premises environments involves several key steps: containerizing your application, configuring environment-specific settings, and using orchestration or service managers to run and scale your solution. In this guide, we'll illustrate two practical deployment scenarios using a sample autonomous agent built with Flask. One example demonstrates deployment to a cloud environment using Docker and a container orchestration tool, and the other shows how to deploy on-premises using a systemd service.

Cloud Deployment with Docker

Using Docker to containerize your AI agent simplifies deployment across various cloud platforms such as AWS, Azure, or Google Cloud. Containerization ensures that your application, along with all its dependencies, runs consistently regardless of the underlying infrastructure.

Step 1: Creating a Sample Flask AI Agent

Consider a simple Flask application that serves as an autonomous agent. Save the following code in a file named `app.py`:

```python
python

# app.py
import os
from flask import Flask, request, jsonify
import openai

app = Flask(__name__)

# Set the OpenAI API key from environment variables
openai.api_key = os.getenv("OPENAI_API_KEY",
"your_default_api_key")

@app.route('/query', methods=['POST'])
def query():
    data = request.get_json()
    user_query = data.get("query", "")
    if not user_query:
        return jsonify({"error": "No query provided"}), 400
    try:
        # Call OpenAI API to generate a response
        response = openai.Completion.create(
            engine="text-davinci-003",
            prompt=f"Answer the following question:
{user_query}",
            max_tokens=150,
            temperature=0.7
        )
        answer = response.choices[0].text.strip()
        return jsonify({"answer": answer}), 200
    except Exception as e:
        return jsonify({"error": str(e)}), 500

if __name__ == '__main__':
    app.run(host="0.0.0.0", port=5000)
```

Explanation:

- This Flask app exposes a `/query` endpoint where users can post a JSON payload containing a query.
- The app calls the OpenAI API and returns the generated response as JSON.
- It reads the API key from an environment variable for secure configuration.

Step 2: Containerizing the Application with Docker

Create a `Dockerfile` to containerize the Flask app:

```
dockerfile

# Use the official Python image as the base image
FROM python:3.9-slim

# Set the working directory in the container
WORKDIR /app

# Copy the requirements file and install dependencies
COPY requirements.txt requirements.txt
RUN pip install --no-cache-dir -r requirements.txt

# Copy the rest of the application code
COPY . .

# Expose port 5000 for the Flask app
EXPOSE 5000

# Define the default command to run the Flask app
CMD ["python", "app.py"]
```

Create a `requirements.txt` file with the necessary dependencies:

```
Flask==2.2.2
openai==0.27.0
```

Explanation:

- The Dockerfile uses a slim Python image, sets up the working directory, installs dependencies, copies your code, exposes the port, and runs the application.
- Using a `requirements.txt` file simplifies dependency management.

Step 3: Building and Running the Docker Container

To build your Docker image, run:

```bash
bash

docker build -t ai-agent .
```

Then, run the container:

```bash
bash

docker run -d -p 5000:5000 --env
OPENAI_API_KEY=your_openai_api_key_here ai-agent
```

Explanation:

- The `docker build` command creates an image tagged `ai-agent`.
- The `docker run` command starts the container in detached mode, maps port 5000, and passes the OpenAI API key as an environment variable.

Step 4: Deploying to a Cloud Platform

You can now deploy your Docker container to any cloud service that supports containers. For example, you can push your Docker image to Docker Hub and deploy it on AWS ECS or Google Kubernetes Engine (GKE).

Example: Pushing to Docker Hub

```bash
bash

docker tag ai-agent your_dockerhub_username/ai-agent:latest
docker push your_dockerhub_username/ai-agent:latest
```

Once pushed, use your chosen cloud provider's container orchestration service to run the container. Cloud platforms often provide web interfaces or CLI tools to manage these deployments.

On-Premises Deployment with systemd

For organizations with strict data control or compliance requirements, on-premises deployment provides complete control over hardware and network configurations. Using systemd, you can manage your AI agent as a service on a Linux server.

Step 1: Prepare Your Application

Ensure that your Flask application (`app.py`) is ready and that you have a virtual environment set up with all dependencies installed.

Step 2: Create a systemd Service File

```
[Unit]
```

```
Description=AI Agent Flask Application
After=network.target

[Service]
User=your_username
Group=your_group
WorkingDirectory=/path/to/your/project
ExecStart=/path/to/your/project/myenv/bin/python app.py
Environment="OPENAI_API_KEY=your_openai_api_key_here"
Restart=always

[Install]
WantedBy=multi-user.target
```

Explanation:

- **Description:** Provides a brief description of the service.
- **After=network.target:** Ensures the service starts after the network is available.
- **User/Group:** Runs the service under a specific user and group.
- **WorkingDirectory:** The directory where your application resides.
- **ExecStart:** Specifies the command to run your application using the virtual environment's Python interpreter.
- **Environment:** Sets necessary environment variables.
- **Restart=always:** Ensures the service restarts automatically if it fails.

Step 3: Start and Enable the Service

Reload systemd to recognize the new service, then start and enable it:

```bash
sudo systemctl daemon-reload
sudo systemctl start ai-agent.service
sudo systemctl enable ai-agent.service
```

Check the status of your service:

```bash
sudo systemctl status ai-agent.service
```

Explanation:

- `daemon-reload` refreshes systemd's configuration.

153

- `start` begins running your service.
- `enable` configures the service to start automatically on boot.
- `status` provides real-time information about the service's state.

Deploying AI agents in both cloud and on-premises environments requires different strategies but shares the common goal of ensuring consistent, scalable, and reliable operations. The cloud deployment example leverages Docker to create a portable container, making it easy to deploy across various cloud platforms. In contrast, the on-premises example uses systemd to manage the service directly on a Linux server, offering complete control over the environment.

Both approaches have their advantages: cloud deployments provide flexibility and scalability with minimal hardware investment, while on-premises deployments offer enhanced security and control. The real-world code examples provided in this guide illustrate practical steps you can implement immediately. As you scale your projects, choose the deployment strategy that best aligns with your operational needs and security requirements, and continuously monitor your deployment to ensure optimal performance.

6.2 CI/CD Strategies for Autonomous Systems

CI/CD (Continuous Integration and Continuous Deployment) strategies are essential for maintaining the reliability and quality of autonomous systems. By automating the build, testing, and deployment processes, you ensure that any changes to your code are validated and deployed quickly, reducing the risk of errors in production. This guide provides a detailed, step-by-step approach to setting up a CI/CD pipeline using GitHub Actions, along with practical code examples that you can implement in real-world projects.

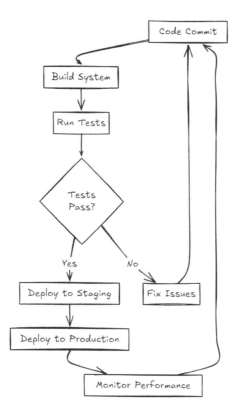

1. Overview

CI/CD pipelines automate the integration of code changes, running tests, building artifacts, and deploying applications. For autonomous systems, which may comprise multiple interacting components, CI/CD helps maintain system stability and encourages continuous improvement. The key benefits include:

- **Early Bug Detection:** Automated tests catch issues as soon as changes are made.
- **Consistent Deployments:** Automated builds reduce the chance of human error.
- **Faster Iteration:** Teams can quickly iterate on features with rapid feedback loops.
- **Scalability:** As your system grows, the pipeline can be extended to cover new services and modules.

2. Setting Up a CI/CD Pipeline with GitHub Actions

GitHub Actions is a popular tool for implementing CI/CD because it integrates directly with your GitHub repository. The following example demonstrates how to set up a pipeline for a simple autonomous system built with Flask.

Step-by-Step Setup

2.1 Create a GitHub Actions Workflow File

Create a file named `.github/workflows/ci.yml` in your repository. This YAML file will define the steps of your CI/CD pipeline.

```yaml
yaml

name: CI/CD Pipeline

on:
  push:
    branches: [ main ]
  pull_request:
    branches: [ main ]

jobs:
  build:
    runs-on: ubuntu-latest

    steps:
    - name: Checkout Repository
      uses: actions/checkout@v3

    - name: Set up Python 3.9
      uses: actions/setup-python@v4
      with:
        python-version: '3.9'

    - name: Install Dependencies
      run: |
        python -m pip install --upgrade pip
        pip install -r requirements.txt

    - name: Run Unit Tests
      run: |
        python -m unittest discover -s tests

    - name: Lint Code with Flake8
```

```
      run: |
        pip install flake8
        flake8 .

  - name: Build Docker Image
    run: |
      docker build -t ai-agent .

  - name: Push Docker Image
    if: github.ref == 'refs/heads/main'
    env:
      DOCKER_USERNAME: ${{ secrets.DOCKER_USERNAME }}
      DOCKER_PASSWORD: ${{ secrets.DOCKER_PASSWORD }}
    run: |
      echo "$DOCKER_PASSWORD" | docker login -u
"$DOCKER_USERNAME" --password-stdin
      docker tag ai-agent your_dockerhub_username/ai-
agent:latest
      docker push your_dockerhub_username/ai-agent:latest
```

Explanation:

- **Triggering the Pipeline:** The workflow triggers on pushes and pull requests to the `main` branch.
- **Checkout:** Uses the `actions/checkout` action to retrieve the repository.
- **Python Setup:** Uses `actions/setup-python` to set up the correct Python version.
- **Dependencies Installation:** Installs required packages from `requirements.txt`.
- **Testing and Linting:** Runs unit tests and code linting with Flake8 to ensure code quality.
- **Docker Build and Push:** Builds a Docker image and, if on the main branch, pushes it to Docker Hub using credentials stored in GitHub Secrets.

3. Running Tests and Automated Builds

Automated testing is a cornerstone of CI/CD. It ensures that new code does not break existing functionality.

Example: Unit Test Execution

Suppose your autonomous system includes a module for processing user queries. A simple test might look like this:

```python
python

# tests/test_query_processor.py
import unittest
from query_processor import process_query  # Assume this
function is defined in query_processor.py

class TestQueryProcessor(unittest.TestCase):
    def test_valid_query(self):
        query = "What is AI?"
        result = process_query(query)
        self.assertIn("Artificial Intelligence", result)

    def test_empty_query(self):
        with self.assertRaises(ValueError):
            process_query("")

if __name__ == "__main__":
    unittest.main()
```

Explanation:

- The test suite checks that a valid query produces a response containing expected text and that an empty query raises an error.
- These tests are automatically executed in the CI/CD pipeline, ensuring that any code changes maintain expected behavior.

---

4. Deployment Strategies within CI/CD

Automated deployment is the final step in the pipeline. Whether deploying to the cloud or on-premises, the pipeline should package and deploy your application consistently.

Example: Deploying a Flask Application with Docker

The workflow file provided in Section 2.1 includes steps to build and push a Docker image. For cloud deployment, you might use services like AWS ECS, Google Kubernetes Engine, or Azure Container Instances. For on-premises deployment, you might integrate with a private Docker registry and deploy using Kubernetes or systemd services.

Commentary:
Automating deployment reduces human error and ensures that every release is built and deployed in a consistent manner. By using Docker, you package your application with all its dependencies, making it portable and easier to run in any environment.

5. Best Practices for CI/CD in Autonomous Systems

- **Incremental Testing:**
  Run tests for individual modules (unit tests) and for the integrated system (integration tests) to catch issues early.
- **Fast Feedback:**
  Keep your test suites fast so that developers receive immediate feedback on changes. This encourages a culture of continuous improvement.
- **Environment Parity:**
  Ensure that the environment used in CI/CD closely mirrors the production environment. Using Docker helps achieve this consistency.
- **Secure Secrets Management:**
  Use secure storage for API keys and other sensitive data. GitHub Secrets is a reliable solution for this purpose.
- **Automated Rollbacks:**
  Consider implementing rollback strategies so that if a deployment fails, the system automatically reverts to the last known good state.
- **Monitoring and Alerts:**
  Integrate monitoring tools within your CI/CD pipeline to alert you when performance metrics or error rates exceed thresholds. This proactive approach can prevent small issues from escalating.

Implementing robust CI/CD strategies is vital for the success of autonomous systems. By automating testing, building, and deployment processes, you ensure that your system remains reliable and can quickly adapt to new changes. The examples provided—ranging from GitHub Actions workflows and unit tests to Docker-based deployments—demonstrate practical, real-world implementations that you can immediately apply in your projects.

These strategies not only enhance the quality and stability of your system but also foster a development culture that values continuous improvement and rapid iteration. With a well-structured CI/CD pipeline in place, you can confidently scale your autonomous systems and respond quickly to any challenges, ensuring that your projects remain robust, secure, and high-performing. Enjoy leveraging these techniques to streamline your development process and deliver exceptional autonomous solutions.

6.3 Monitoring, Logging, and Analytics for Agent Performance

Monitoring, logging, and analytics are vital components for ensuring that your autonomous agent systems perform reliably and efficiently in production. By capturing detailed metrics and logs, you can detect performance issues, diagnose errors, and continuously improve your system. This guide explains how to set up robust monitoring and logging mechanisms, and how to analyze collected data for actionable insights. The examples provided use Python and common tools like the built-in logging module and the Prometheus Python client for real-world applicability.

1. Setting Up Comprehensive Logging

Logging captures detailed records of your system's operations. A well-configured logging system can help you trace execution flow, diagnose errors, and monitor key events. The Python built-in logging module is a robust solution for this purpose.

Step 1: Configure the Logging System

Below is an example that configures logging to output messages both to a file and to the console. This setup is useful for local debugging and for persisting logs in production.

```python
import logging

# Configure logging settings
```

```
logging.basicConfig(
    level=logging.DEBUG,  # Capture all levels of log
messages
    format="%(asctime)s [%(levelname)s] %(name)s:
%(message)s",
    handlers=[
        logging.FileHandler("agent_performance.log"),  # Log
to a file
        logging.StreamHandler()  # Also output logs to the
console
    ]
)

logger = logging.getLogger("AgentMonitor")
logger.info("Logging system initialized.")
```

Explanation:

- **Logging Level:** Setting the level to DEBUG ensures that all types of messages are recorded.
- **Format:** The log format includes the timestamp, log level, logger name, and message.
- **Handlers:** Logs are directed to both a file (`agent_performance.log`) and the console, providing persistence and real-time monitoring.

---

2. Monitoring Agent Performance with Prometheus

For real-time performance monitoring, Prometheus is a popular choice. The Prometheus Python client enables you to collect metrics such as request durations, error rates, and throughput.

Step 1: Install the Prometheus Client

```bash
pip install prometheus_client
```

Step 2: Set Up a Prometheus Metrics Endpoint

Below is an example Flask application that integrates Prometheus metrics. The example includes a counter for tracking the number of processed queries and a histogram to record response times.

161

```python
from flask import Flask, request, jsonify
from prometheus_client import Counter, Histogram,
generate_latest, CONTENT_TYPE_LATEST
import time
import random

app = Flask(__name__)

# Define Prometheus metrics
QUERY_COUNT = Counter('agent_query_count', 'Total number of
queries processed')
RESPONSE_TIME = Histogram('agent_response_time_seconds',
'Response time for processing queries')

@app.route('/metrics')
def metrics():
    """
    Expose Prometheus metrics.
    """
    return generate_latest(), 200, {'Content-Type':
CONTENT_TYPE_LATEST}

@app.route('/process', methods=['POST'])
def process_query():
    """
    Process a query and return a simulated response.
    """
    start_time = time.time()
    QUERY_COUNT.inc()  # Increment the query counter

    data = request.get_json()
    query = data.get("query", "")

    if not query:
        response = {"error": "No query provided"}
        status = 400
    else:
        # Simulate processing delay
        time.sleep(random.uniform(0.1, 0.5))
        response = {"answer": query.upper()}
        status = 200

    elapsed_time = time.time() - start_time
    RESPONSE_TIME.observe(elapsed_time)  # Record the elapsed
time

    return jsonify(response), status

if __name__ == '__main__':
```

```
    app.run(host="0.0.0.0", port=5000, debug=True)
```

Explanation:

- **Metrics Definition:**
  - `QUERY_COUNT` is a counter that increments each time a query is processed.
  - `RESPONSE_TIME` is a histogram that records the time taken to process each query.
- **Metrics Endpoint:** The `/metrics` route exposes the metrics in a format that Prometheus can scrape.
- **Processing Endpoint:** The `/process` route simulates processing a query. It measures the time taken for each request and updates the corresponding metrics.
- **Simulated Response:** For simplicity, the agent transforms the query to uppercase. In a real system, this would be replaced with actual processing logic.

---

3. Logging and Monitoring Combined

Integrating logging with monitoring provides a complete picture of system behavior. While Prometheus collects quantitative metrics, logs capture detailed context and errors.

Example: Logging Errors and Performance Data

Enhance the previous Flask application to log error conditions and performance anomalies.

```python
import logging
from flask import Flask, request, jsonify
from prometheus_client import Counter, Histogram,
generate_latest, CONTENT_TYPE_LATEST
import time
import random

# Set up logging
logging.basicConfig(
    level=logging.DEBUG,
```

```python
    format="%(asctime)s [%(levelname)s] %(name)s:
%(message)s",
    handlers=[
        logging.FileHandler("agent_performance.log"),
        logging.StreamHandler()
    ]
)
logger = logging.getLogger("AgentMonitor")

app = Flask(__name__)

# Define Prometheus metrics
QUERY_COUNT = Counter('agent_query_count', 'Total number of
queries processed')
RESPONSE_TIME = Histogram('agent_response_time_seconds',
'Response time for processing queries')

@app.route('/metrics')
def metrics():
    return generate_latest(), 200, {'Content-Type':
CONTENT_TYPE_LATEST}

@app.route('/process', methods=['POST'])
def process_query():
    start_time = time.time()
    QUERY_COUNT.inc()
    data = request.get_json()
    query = data.get("query", "")

    if not query:
        logger.warning("Received empty query.")
        response = {"error": "No query provided"}
        status = 400
    else:
        try:
            # Simulate processing delay and possible random
error
            time.sleep(random.uniform(0.1, 0.5))
            if random.random() < 0.1:  # 10% chance to
simulate an error
                raise ValueError("Simulated processing
error.")
            processed = query.upper()
            response = {"answer": processed}
            status = 200
        except Exception as e:
            logger.error(f"Error processing query '{query}':
{e}", exc_info=True)
            response = {"error": "An error occurred during
processing."}
            status = 500
```

```
    elapsed_time = time.time() - start_time
    RESPONSE_TIME.observe(elapsed_time)
    logger.debug(f"Processed query in {elapsed_time:.3f}
seconds.")
    return jsonify(response), status

if __name__ == '__main__':
    app.run(host="0.0.0.0", port=5000, debug=True)
```

Explanation:

- **Error Logging:**
  - If a query is empty or an exception is raised, the error is logged with context.
- **Performance Logging:**
  - The time taken to process each query is logged, helping you identify performance bottlenecks.
- **Simulated Error:**
  - A random error is simulated to demonstrate error handling and logging.

Effective monitoring, logging, and analytics are essential for maintaining high performance in autonomous agent systems. The examples provided illustrate how to integrate Python's logging module with Prometheus metrics in a Flask application. This setup enables you to capture both granular log details and high-level performance metrics, providing a comprehensive view of system health.

By continuously monitoring these metrics and analyzing logs, you can quickly identify issues, optimize performance, and ensure that your agents operate reliably under varying conditions. This holistic approach to monitoring not only supports immediate troubleshooting but also informs long-term improvements and scalability strategies.

6.4 Maintenance, Updates, and Lifecycle Management

Monitoring, logging, and analytics are vital components for ensuring that your autonomous agent systems perform reliably and efficiently in production. By capturing detailed metrics and logs, you can detect performance issues, diagnose errors, and continuously improve your system. This guide explains how to set up robust monitoring and logging mechanisms, and how to analyze collected data for actionable insights. The examples provided use Python and common tools like the built-in logging module and the Prometheus Python client for real-world applicability.

1. Setting Up Comprehensive Logging

Logging captures detailed records of your system's operations. A well-configured logging system can help you trace execution flow, diagnose errors, and monitor key events. The Python built-in logging module is a robust solution for this purpose.

Step 1: Configure the Logging System

Below is an example that configures logging to output messages both to a file and to the console. This setup is useful for local debugging and for persisting logs in production.

```python
import logging

# Configure logging settings
logging.basicConfig(
    level=logging.DEBUG,   # Capture all levels of log messages
    format="%(asctime)s [%(levelname)s] %(name)s: %(message)s",
    handlers=[
        logging.FileHandler("agent_performance.log"),   # Log to a file
        logging.StreamHandler()   # Also output logs to the console
    ]
)

logger = logging.getLogger("AgentMonitor")
logger.info("Logging system initialized.")
```

Explanation:

- **Logging Level:** Setting the level to DEBUG ensures that all types of messages are recorded.
- **Format:** The log format includes the timestamp, log level, logger name, and message.
- **Handlers:** Logs are directed to both a file (`agent_performance.log`) and the console, providing persistence and real-time monitoring.

2. Monitoring Agent Performance with Prometheus

For real-time performance monitoring, Prometheus is a popular choice. The Prometheus Python client enables you to collect metrics such as request durations, error rates, and throughput.

Step 1: Install the Prometheus Client

```bash
pip install prometheus_client
```

Step 2: Set Up a Prometheus Metrics Endpoint

Below is an example Flask application that integrates Prometheus metrics. The example includes a counter for tracking the number of processed queries and a histogram to record response times.

```python
from flask import Flask, request, jsonify
from prometheus_client import Counter, Histogram,
generate_latest, CONTENT_TYPE_LATEST
import time
import random

app = Flask(__name__)

# Define Prometheus metrics
QUERY_COUNT = Counter('agent_query_count', 'Total number of
queries processed')
RESPONSE_TIME = Histogram('agent_response_time_seconds',
'Response time for processing queries')

@app.route('/metrics')
```

```
def metrics():
    """
    Expose Prometheus metrics.
    """
    return generate_latest(), 200, {'Content-Type':
CONTENT_TYPE_LATEST}

@app.route('/process', methods=['POST'])
def process_query():
    """
    Process a query and return a simulated response.
    """
    start_time = time.time()
    QUERY_COUNT.inc()  # Increment the query counter

    data = request.get_json()
    query = data.get("query", "")

    if not query:
        response = {"error": "No query provided"}
        status = 400
    else:
        # Simulate processing delay
        time.sleep(random.uniform(0.1, 0.5))
        response = {"answer": query.upper()}
        status = 200

    elapsed_time = time.time() - start_time
    RESPONSE_TIME.observe(elapsed_time)  # Record the elapsed
time

    return jsonify(response), status

if __name__ == '__main__':
    app.run(host="0.0.0.0", port=5000, debug=True)
```

Explanation:

- **Metrics Definition:**
  - `QUERY_COUNT` is a counter that increments each time a query is processed.
  - `RESPONSE_TIME` is a histogram that records the time taken to process each query.
- **Metrics Endpoint:** The `/metrics` route exposes the metrics in a format that Prometheus can scrape.
- **Processing Endpoint:** The `/process` route simulates processing a query. It measures the time taken for each request and updates the corresponding metrics.

- **Simulated Response:** For simplicity, the agent transforms the query to uppercase. In a real system, this would be replaced with actual processing logic.

---

3. Logging and Monitoring Combined

Integrating logging with monitoring provides a complete picture of system behavior. While Prometheus collects quantitative metrics, logs capture detailed context and errors.

Example: Logging Errors and Performance Data

Enhance the previous Flask application to log error conditions and performance anomalies.

```python
python

import logging
from flask import Flask, request, jsonify
from prometheus_client import Counter, Histogram,
generate_latest, CONTENT_TYPE_LATEST
import time
import random

# Set up logging
logging.basicConfig(
    level=logging.DEBUG,
    format="%(asctime)s [%(levelname)s] %(name)s:
%(message)s",
    handlers=[
        logging.FileHandler("agent_performance.log"),
        logging.StreamHandler()
    ]
)
logger = logging.getLogger("AgentMonitor")

app = Flask(__name__)

# Define Prometheus metrics
QUERY_COUNT = Counter('agent_query_count', 'Total number of
queries processed')
RESPONSE_TIME = Histogram('agent_response_time_seconds',
'Response time for processing queries')

@app.route('/metrics')
```

```
def metrics():
    return generate_latest(), 200, {'Content-Type':
CONTENT_TYPE_LATEST}

@app.route('/process', methods=['POST'])
def process_query():
    start_time = time.time()
    QUERY_COUNT.inc()
    data = request.get_json()
    query = data.get("query", "")

    if not query:
        logger.warning("Received empty query.")
        response = {"error": "No query provided"}
        status = 400
    else:
        try:
            # Simulate processing delay and possible random
error
            time.sleep(random.uniform(0.1, 0.5))
            if random.random() < 0.1:   # 10% chance to
simulate an error
                raise ValueError("Simulated processing
error.")
            processed = query.upper()
            response = {"answer": processed}
            status = 200
        except Exception as e:
            logger.error(f"Error processing query '{query}':
{e}", exc_info=True)
            response = {"error": "An error occurred during
processing."}
            status = 500

    elapsed_time = time.time() - start_time
    RESPONSE_TIME.observe(elapsed_time)
    logger.debug(f"Processed query in {elapsed_time:.3f}
seconds.")
    return jsonify(response), status

if __name__ == '__main__':
    app.run(host="0.0.0.0", port=5000, debug=True)
```

Explanation:

- **Error Logging:**
  - If a query is empty or an exception is raised, the error is logged with context.
- **Performance Logging:**

- The time taken to process each query is logged, helping you identify performance bottlenecks.
- **Simulated Error:**
  - A random error is simulated to demonstrate error handling and logging.

Effective monitoring, logging, and analytics are essential for maintaining high performance in autonomous agent systems. The examples provided illustrate how to integrate Python's logging module with Prometheus metrics in a Flask application. This setup enables you to capture both granular log details and high-level performance metrics, providing a comprehensive view of system health.

By continuously monitoring these metrics and analyzing logs, you can quickly identify issues, optimize performance, and ensure that your agents operate reliably under varying conditions. This holistic approach to monitoring not only supports immediate troubleshooting but also informs long-term improvements and scalability strategies.

Chapter 7: The Future of AI Agents

The future of AI agents is both exciting and complex, blending breakthroughs in technology with evolving societal needs. As we look ahead, the landscape is set to change dramatically through emerging trends, innovative architectures, and a commitment to continuous learning. This chapter explores these themes, providing a roadmap for staying at the forefront of autonomous AI development.

7.1 Emerging Trends and Innovations in Autonomous AI

Emerging trends in autonomous AI are reshaping the way systems learn, adapt, and interact with the world. One notable development is the shift toward multimodal models that can process not only text but also images, audio, and even sensor data. These models allow AI agents to gain a richer understanding of their environment, much like a human who listens, observes, and reads simultaneously to form a complete picture. This trend is driving the creation of more context-aware systems that can support applications from healthcare diagnostics to autonomous driving.

Another major trend is continuous and federated learning. Instead of training large models in a centralized manner, federated learning enables devices at the edge—like smartphones or IoT sensors—to collaboratively learn without sharing raw data. This not only enhances privacy but also allows models to be updated in real time based on local interactions. Imagine a fleet of autonomous vehicles that continuously learns from each other's experiences without compromising individual data privacy. Such systems promise greater adaptability and resilience in dynamic environments.

The integration of specialized AI agents for niche tasks is also on the rise. Early AI systems were often generalists, but the future belongs to agents that excel in specific domains—whether it's a legal assistant that understands intricate regulatory language or a medical diagnostic tool that can parse radiological images with high accuracy. This specialization is supported by advancements in transfer learning and model fine-tuning, which allow developers to start with a general model and tailor it to a specific use case with relatively little additional data.

Innovation is further propelled by the emergence of tool-augmented AI, where autonomous agents are not just standalone models but are equipped with external tools and plugins to extend their capabilities. For instance, agents can now integrate with web browsers, databases, and other APIs to perform tasks ranging from complex data analysis to real-time decision-making. This modular approach transforms AI agents into versatile platforms that can be dynamically configured to meet a wide range of operational needs.

Edge computing is another transformative trend. By processing data locally on devices, edge computing reduces latency and bandwidth usage, making AI applications more responsive and reliable—critical factors for time-sensitive tasks like emergency response or industrial automation. In such architectures, the combination of powerful local processing and centralized cloud-based analytics creates a hybrid system that leverages the best of both worlds.

The push for ethical and transparent AI is also influencing the design of autonomous systems. Researchers and practitioners are increasingly focused on explainability, ensuring that AI decisions can be understood and scrutinized by humans. This involves developing methods for model interpretability and bias mitigation, as well as embedding ethical guidelines into the system's core architecture. These measures are crucial for fostering trust and ensuring that AI systems operate fairly in real-world scenarios.

Finally, advancements in hardware are set to accelerate the capabilities of autonomous AI. The proliferation of specialized AI accelerators and even early steps toward quantum computing are providing the computational horsepower required to train and run ever more complex models. This hardware evolution is critical for meeting the demands of sophisticated AI agents, enabling them to process larger datasets faster and perform more complex reasoning in real time.

In summary, the future of autonomous AI is characterized by increased multimodality, continuous learning via federated approaches, specialization of agents, integration with external tools, edge computing, a strong focus on ethical practices, and hardware advancements. Each of these trends contributes to building systems that are more adaptive, efficient, and responsible. Staying informed about these innovations—and being prepared to integrate them into your projects—will be key to harnessing the full potential of autonomous AI in the coming years.

7.2 Future Architectures and Next-Generation Tools

Future architectures for autonomous AI agents are set to leverage a blend of modularity, distributed processing, and seamless interoperability to handle increasingly complex tasks. One of the most significant shifts is the move away from monolithic designs toward highly decoupled, service-oriented structures. In these architectures, each component is a self-contained module that communicates with others through well-defined APIs. This modular approach not only simplifies maintenance and updates but also enables scalability, as individual components can be upgraded or scaled independently without impacting the entire system.

Embracing Microservices and Serverless Computing

Modern architectures are gravitating towards microservices and serverless paradigms. Microservices decompose a system into loosely coupled, independently deployable services. Each microservice performs a specific function—such as data ingestion, query processing, or result generation—allowing developers to tailor and scale parts of the system based on demand. Serverless computing, on the other hand, abstracts away the underlying infrastructure so that developers can focus solely on code. This is particularly valuable for autonomous systems that must quickly adapt to fluctuating workloads. For instance, a serverless function might process incoming sensor data and trigger an AI agent's response, only consuming resources when active and scaling automatically during peak usage.

Edge Computing and Federated Learning

The next generation of architectures will increasingly rely on edge computing, where processing is performed close to the data source. This reduces latency and minimizes data transmission costs, which is crucial for applications such as real-time monitoring in industrial automation or smart healthcare. Coupled with edge computing is federated learning, a method where models are trained across multiple decentralized devices without sharing raw data. Federated learning enhances privacy and enables continuous, distributed learning, allowing agents to adapt to local conditions while contributing to a global model.

Interoperability and Integration Frameworks

As AI agents become more specialized, future architectures will need robust frameworks for integrating diverse tools and services. Standardized communication protocols and data formats—such as RESTful APIs and JSON—will be essential to ensure smooth interoperability. Next-generation integration platforms will facilitate the dynamic composition of workflows, allowing agents to interact with external data sources, IoT devices, and third-party services in real time. For example, an AI-driven logistics system might integrate with GPS data, weather APIs, and supply chain databases to optimize delivery routes continuously.

Next-Generation Tools and Platforms

The tools available for building these architectures are also evolving rapidly. Platforms like Kubernetes are already transforming how containerized applications are deployed and managed at scale. In the near future, we can expect even more specialized orchestration tools designed specifically for AI workloads. These platforms will optimize resource allocation for GPU-intensive tasks and provide built-in support for scaling complex, distributed AI models.

Additionally, low-code and visual programming environments are emerging to democratize AI development. These next-generation tools enable developers and even non-experts to design complex workflows through intuitive drag-and-drop interfaces. Such tools not only accelerate development but also facilitate experimentation and rapid prototyping, allowing organizations to iterate quickly and stay ahead of the curve.

Expert Commentary and Real-World Implications

Industry experts emphasize that the future of AI architectures is not just about raw performance, but also about resilience, adaptability, and ethical integration. A robust architecture must be capable of handling failures gracefully—through redundancy, fault tolerance, and dynamic load balancing—while also ensuring that AI decisions are transparent and explainable. In real-world applications, this translates to systems that are both powerful and trustworthy. For example, in financial services, an AI system that leverages microservices for fraud detection can dynamically scale during peak transaction periods and maintain continuous monitoring, while also providing audit trails for regulatory compliance.

Another practical insight is the importance of designing for continuous learning. Future architectures will need to support ongoing model updates and adaptive learning strategies. This means incorporating mechanisms for feedback loops and real-time performance analytics, ensuring that the system evolves as new data becomes available. Organizations that build these capabilities into their AI systems will be better positioned to respond to emerging challenges and leverage new opportunities.

The future architectures and next-generation tools for autonomous AI agents represent a convergence of multiple advanced technologies. By embracing microservices, serverless computing, edge processing, federated learning, and specialized orchestration frameworks, developers can build systems that are scalable, resilient, and highly adaptable. These architectures not only meet the technical demands of tomorrow but also address critical issues like data privacy, real-time responsiveness, and ethical governance. Staying informed about these trends and integrating next-generation tools into your development process will be key to unlocking the full potential of autonomous AI, ensuring that your systems remain at the forefront of innovation while delivering tangible, real-world value.

7.3 Continuous Learning and Staying Ahead in the AI Landscape

Continuous learning in AI systems is an ongoing, dynamic process that goes far beyond simply updating a model every few months. In today's fast-paced AI landscape, staying ahead means continuously refining your models, incorporating user feedback, and adapting to new data sources and techniques. This section explores practical strategies and expert insights on how to design autonomous systems that learn over time and remain relevant as the technology and business environment evolve.

One key aspect of continuous learning is the establishment of robust feedback loops. In a well-designed autonomous system, every interaction is an opportunity to learn. For instance, consider a customer support chatbot that not only answers queries but also records user feedback on its responses. This feedback can be aggregated and used to retrain the model, fine-tuning its performance. By integrating mechanisms to collect feedback—whether through explicit user ratings or implicit behavioral signals such as repeated queries—the system can identify weaknesses and improve over time. Automated retraining pipelines, which periodically update models using the latest data, ensure that the system adapts to emerging trends and new user needs without manual intervention.

Another critical strategy is incremental learning. Instead of overhauling your entire model with each update, focus on incorporating small, frequent improvements. Techniques like transfer learning and online learning are particularly useful here. With transfer learning, you begin with a pre-trained model and adjust it on your specific dataset, reducing training time and computational cost while still capturing new information. Online learning methods allow models to update continuously as new data arrives. This approach is especially beneficial in dynamic environments where the context or user behavior can shift rapidly—for example, in real-time financial forecasting or adaptive content recommendation systems.

Federated learning is an emerging method that also supports continuous learning while addressing privacy concerns. In federated learning, models are trained locally on edge devices and only the updates (not the raw data) are aggregated centrally. This not only reduces latency and bandwidth usage but also ensures that sensitive data remains on the user's device. Imagine a network of smartphones that collectively learn to improve a language model for predictive texting, all while preserving individual privacy. Such decentralized learning methods are likely to become more prominent as data privacy regulations tighten and the need for real-time adaptation grows.

Staying ahead in the AI landscape also requires active engagement with the broader community. Regularly reading research papers, participating in conferences, and contributing to open-source projects are all ways to remain informed about the latest breakthroughs and best practices. Many organizations now maintain internal knowledge bases where lessons learned from past deployments are documented and shared. This culture of continuous improvement, combined with agile development practices, enables teams to quickly iterate on designs and deploy improvements with minimal disruption.

From an operational perspective, continuous monitoring and performance analytics are essential. By tracking key performance indicators (KPIs) such as response times, error rates, and user satisfaction metrics, you can identify areas where the system may be underperforming. Integrating these metrics with automated alerts and dashboards not only helps in diagnosing issues early but also provides actionable insights that inform future training cycles and system optimizations. For example, if analytics reveal that certain types of queries consistently result in errors, those cases can be prioritized in the next model update cycle.

In addition to technical strategies, fostering a culture that values continuous learning is crucial. This means encouraging collaboration between data scientists, engineers, and domain experts to regularly review system performance and share insights. Regularly scheduled reviews and retrospective meetings can lead to incremental improvements that accumulate over time, ensuring that the system evolves in line with both technological advances and changing user requirements.

In summary, continuous learning and staying ahead in the AI landscape require a multifaceted approach that blends technical innovation with organizational best practices. By establishing feedback loops, leveraging incremental and federated learning techniques, and maintaining rigorous performance monitoring, you create a system that not only adapts to new data but also grows more intelligent and efficient over time. Moreover, active engagement with the research community and a culture of continuous improvement are vital for maintaining competitive advantage. This proactive approach ensures that your autonomous agents remain cutting-edge, resilient, and capable of delivering lasting value in an ever-evolving digital world.

Appendices

Appendix A: Glossary of Key Terms

This glossary is intended to serve as a quick reference for important concepts, technologies, and terms related to autonomous agents and AI systems. Understanding these terms is crucial for grasping the technical details and best practices outlined in this book.

Autonomous Agent

A software system capable of operating independently to achieve specific goals, often using artificial intelligence. Autonomous agents make decisions and perform tasks without continuous human intervention.
Example: A chatbot that autonomously processes customer inquiries and provides relevant answers.

API (Application Programming Interface)

A set of protocols and tools that allow different software applications to communicate with one another. APIs facilitate data exchange and enable integration between diverse systems.
Example: A weather application using the OpenWeatherMap API to retrieve current weather conditions.

CI/CD (Continuous Integration/Continuous Deployment)

A set of practices that automate the building, testing, and deployment of software. CI/CD pipelines ensure that code changes are continuously tested and deployed, reducing manual errors and accelerating development cycles.
Example: Using GitHub Actions to automatically run tests and deploy a new version of your AI agent every time code is pushed to the repository.

Containerization

A lightweight form of virtualization that packages an application and its dependencies into a container, ensuring that it runs consistently across different computing environments.
Example: Docker containers are widely used to deploy microservices in cloud environments.

Edge Computing

Processing data near the source of data generation (e.g., on a device or local server) rather than relying on centralized data centers. This reduces latency and improves responsiveness, which is crucial for real-time applications.
Example: Smart sensors in a manufacturing plant that process data on-site to trigger immediate actions.

Federated Learning

A decentralized machine learning approach where multiple devices train a model collaboratively without sharing raw data. Only model updates are aggregated centrally, enhancing data privacy and reducing bandwidth requirements.
Example: Smartphones collaboratively training a predictive text model while keeping user data local.

LLM (Large Language Model)

A type of AI model that has been trained on vast amounts of text data and can generate human-like language. LLMs are used for tasks such as natural language understanding and generation.
Example: OpenAI's GPT-4, which can understand and generate text based on complex prompts.

Logging

The practice of recording detailed information about system operations, including errors, warnings, and informational events. Logs are essential for debugging, monitoring, and auditing system behavior.
Example: A log file that records each query processed by an AI agent, along with its response time and any errors encountered.

Microservices

An architectural style that structures an application as a collection of loosely coupled, independently deployable services. Each service is responsible for a specific functionality and communicates with others through APIs.
Example: A customer support system where one microservice handles user queries, another manages database interactions, and a third handles notifications.

Orchestration

The automated coordination and management of multiple services or components in a system. In the context of autonomous agents, orchestration ensures that tasks are distributed appropriately and that different agents work together cohesively.
Example: Using Kubernetes to manage and scale Docker containers running different parts of an AI system.

Prompt Engineering

The process of designing and refining prompts to elicit desired responses from language models. Effective prompt engineering can significantly improve the accuracy and relevance of AI-generated outputs.
Example: Crafting a detailed prompt that instructs an AI to summarize a piece of text in a specific style.

Scalability

The ability of a system to handle increasing workloads by expanding its resources. Scalability can be achieved through vertical scaling (adding more power to a single machine) or horizontal scaling (adding more machines to distribute the load).
Example: Deploying an autonomous system on a cloud platform that automatically provisions additional instances as demand grows.

Serverless Computing

A cloud computing model where the cloud provider dynamically manages the allocation of machine resources. Developers write code without worrying about server management, and resources scale automatically based on demand.
Example: AWS Lambda functions that run code in response to events without the need for provisioning servers.

Virtual Environment

An isolated environment that allows you to manage dependencies and packages for a specific project without affecting the global Python installation.

Example: Using `venv` or `conda` to create a dedicated workspace for your autonomous agent project.

Appendix B: Detailed Installation and Setup Guides

This appendix provides step-by-step guides for installing and setting up the various tools and frameworks discussed in the book. Following these guides will help you create a consistent and robust development environment for building autonomous AI systems.

B.1 Setting Up Your Python Environment

Install Python:
Download and install Python 3.7 or higher from the official Python website. Verify the installation with:

```
python --version
```

Create a Virtual Environment:
Use the built-in `venv` module to create an isolated environment:

```
python -m venv myenv
```

Activate the environment:

On Windows:

```
myenv\Scripts\activate
```

On macOS/Linux:

```
source myenv/bin/activate
```

Install Essential Packages:
Create a `requirements.txt` file listing your dependencies, for example:

```
Flask==2.2.2
openai==0.27.0
langchain==0.0.135
llama-index==0.5.8
prometheus_client==0.14.1
```

```
python-dotenv==0.21.0
```

Install dependencies:

```
pip install -r requirements.txt
```

Commentary:
Setting up a virtual environment ensures that your project dependencies are isolated, preventing conflicts with other projects. This foundational step is crucial for reproducibility and long-term maintainability.

B.2 Installing and Configuring Docker

Install Docker:
Download and install Docker from the official Docker website. Follow the installation instructions for your operating system.

Verify Installation:
Open a terminal and run:

```
docker --version
```

This should display the installed Docker version.

Create a Dockerfile for Your Application:
In your project directory, create a `Dockerfile`:

```
FROM python:3.9-slim
WORKDIR /app
COPY requirements.txt requirements.txt
RUN pip install --no-cache-dir -r requirements.txt
COPY . .
EXPOSE 5000
CMD ["python", "app.py"]
```

Build and run the container:

```
docker build -t ai-agent .
docker run -d -p 5000:5000 --env
OPENAI_API_KEY=your_openai_api_key_here ai-agent
```

Commentary:
Containerizing your application with Docker ensures consistent execution across different environments, whether on your local machine, in a test environment, or in production.

B.3 Setting Up GitHub Actions for CI/CD

1. **Create a Workflow File:**
   In your repository, create `.github/workflows/ci.yml`:

```yaml
name: CI/CD Pipeline

on:
  push:
    branches: [ main ]
  pull_request:
    branches: [ main ]

jobs:
  build:
    runs-on: ubuntu-latest
    steps:
      - name: Checkout Repository
        uses: actions/checkout@v3
      - name: Set up Python 3.9
        uses: actions/setup-python@v4
        with:
          python-version: '3.9'
      - name: Install Dependencies
        run: |
          python -m pip install --upgrade pip
          pip install -r requirements.txt
      - name: Run Tests
        run: |
          python -m unittest discover -s tests
      - name: Build Docker Image
        run: |
          docker build -t ai-agent .
      - name: Push Docker Image
        if: github.ref == 'refs/heads/main'
        env:
          DOCKER_USERNAME: ${{ secrets.DOCKER_USERNAME }}
          DOCKER_PASSWORD: ${{ secrets.DOCKER_PASSWORD }}
        run: |
          echo "$DOCKER_PASSWORD" | docker login -u
"$DOCKER_USERNAME" --password-stdin
```

```
        docker tag ai-agent your_dockerhub_username/ai-
agent:latest
        docker push your_dockerhub_username/ai-agent:latest
```

Configure Secrets:
In your GitHub repository settings, add the secrets `DOCKER_USERNAME` and `DOCKER_PASSWORD`.

Commentary:
This CI/CD pipeline automatically checks out your code, sets up the environment, runs tests, builds the Docker image, and pushes it to Docker Hub when changes are made to the main branch. Automating these tasks helps maintain code quality and speeds up deployment.

B.4 Setting Up Monitoring and Logging Tools

Install Prometheus Client:
Use pip to install the Prometheus client library:

```
pip install prometheus_client
```

Configure Metrics in Your Application:
Add a `/metrics` endpoint to your Flask application to expose metrics:

```
from prometheus_client import Counter, Histogram,
generate_latest, CONTENT_TYPE_LATEST
from flask import Flask, Response

app = Flask(__name__)
QUERY_COUNT = Counter('agent_query_count', 'Total number of
queries processed')
RESPONSE_TIME = Histogram('agent_response_time_seconds',
'Response time for processing queries')

@app.route('/metrics')
def metrics():
    return Response(generate_latest(),
mimetype=CONTENT_TYPE_LATEST)
```

Commentary:
Monitoring endpoints allow you to integrate with Prometheus and Grafana to visualize performance and system health, providing continuous insights into your application's behavior.

185

B.5 Detailed Installation Guides for Specific Tools

For each tool mentioned in this book, refer to the following installation steps:

LangChain:

```
pip install langchain
```

Refer to LangChain's GitHub repository for detailed documentation.

CrewAI:

```
pip install crewai
```

Consult the official documentation for setup and configuration options.

AutoGen:

```
pip install autogen
```

Follow the setup guide provided by the project maintainers for API integration and custom agent configuration.

LlamaIndex:

```
pip install llama-index
```

Detailed installation and configuration instructions are available on the LlamaIndex GitHub page.

GPT Engineer:

```
pip install gpt-engineer openai
```

Check out the official repository for usage examples and troubleshooting tips.

Semantic Kernel:

```
pip install semantic-kernel
```

The Semantic Kernel documentation provides comprehensive guidance on integrating with LLMs.

SuperAGI:

```
pip install superagi
```

Follow the detailed guide provided by the SuperAGI project for best practices in production deployments.

LangFlow:

```
pip install langflow
```

Use the command `langflow` to launch the visual interface and refer to the LangFlow documentation for workflow design.

AgentGPT:

```
pip install agentgpt
```

The project's documentation offers step-by-step instructions for configuring and deploying AgentGPT through a browser-based interface.

DevOpsGPT:

```
pip install devopsgpt openai
```

Detailed setup instructions are available in the DevOpsGPT documentation, guiding you through automated configuration and deployment processes.

Commentary:
Each tool has its own ecosystem and documentation. Using these detailed guides will ensure that you set up each component correctly and can integrate them smoothly into your autonomous system. Keeping your environment updated and following best practices for installation will save time and prevent issues during later stages of development.